CONGRESSIONAL POLICIES, PRACTICES AND PROCEDURES

EARMARKS: DISCLOSURE, LEGAL DEVELOPMENTS AND TRANSPORTATION FUNDING

CONGRESSIONAL POLICIES, PRACTICES AND PROCEDURES

Additional books in this series can be found on Nova's website under the Series tab.

Additional E-books in this series can be found on Nova's website under the E-books tab.

CONGRESSIONAL POLICIES, PRACTICES AND PROCEDURES

EARMARKS: DISCLOSURE, LEGAL DEVELOPMENTS AND TRANSPORTATION FUNDING

ROGER D. HALSTEAD
EDITOR

Nova Science Publishers, Inc.
New York

For permission to use material from this book please contact us:
Telephone 631-231-7269; Fax 631-231-8175
Web Site: http://www.novapublishers.com

Additional color graphics may be available in the e-book version of this book.

Library of Congress Cataloging-in-Publication Data

Earmarks : disclosure, legal developments and transportation funding / editors, Roger D. Halstead.
p. cm.
Consists of reprints of reports prepared by the Congressional Research Service.
Includes bibliographical references and index.
ISBN 978-1-61324-588-0 (softcover : alk. paper) 1. Budget--Law and legislation--United States. 2. Legislation--United States. 3. United States. Congress--Rules and practice. 4. United States--Appropriations and expenditures. I. Halstead, Roger D. II. Library of Congress. Congressional Research Service.
KF6221.A56E17 2011
343.73'034--dc22

2011014474

Published by Nova Science Publishers, Inc. New York

CONTENTS

Preface		**ix**
Chapter 1	Earmark Disclosure Rules in the House: Member and Committee Requirements *Megan Suzanne Lynch*	**1**
Chapter 2	Earmark Disclosure Rules in the Senate: Member and Committee Requirements *Megan Suzanne Lynch*	**9**
Chapter 3	House and Senate Procedural Rules Concerning Earmark Disclosure *Sandy Streeter*	**17**
Chapter 4	Earmarks Executive Order: Legal Issues *Thomas J. Nicola and T.J. Halstead*	**33**
Chapter 5	Earmarks Disclosed by Congress: FY2008-FY2010 Regular Appropriations Bills *Carol Hardy Vincent and Jim Monke*	**49**
Chapter 6	Transportation Spending under an Earmark Ban *Robert S. Kirk, William J. Mallett and David Randall Peterman*	**77**
Index		**93**

PREFACE

Earmark disclosure rules in both the House and Senate were implemented with the stated intention of bringing more transparency to congressionally directed spending. The administrative responsibilities associated with these rules vary by chamber. This book outlines the major administrative responsibilities of Members and committees of the House of Representative and the Senate associated with the chamber's earmark disclosure rules.

Chapter 1- Earmark disclosure rules in both the House and Senate establish certain administrative responsibilities that vary by chamber. Under House rules, a Member requesting that an earmark be included in legislation is responsible for providing specific written information, such as the purpose and recipient of the earmark, to the committee of jurisdiction. Further, House committees are responsible for compiling, presenting, and maintaining such requests in accord with House rules. In the House, disclosure rules apply to any congressional earmark, limited tax benefit, or limited tariff benefit included in either the text of a bill or any report accompanying the measure, including a conference report and joint explanatory statement. The disclosure requirements apply to earmarks in appropriations legislation, authorizing legislation, and tax measures. Furthermore they apply not only to measures reported by committees, but also to measures not reported by committees, "manager's amendments," and conference reports.

Chapter 2- Earmark disclosure rules in both the House and Senate establish certain administrative responsibilities that vary by chamber. Under Senate rules, a Senator requesting that an earmark be included in legislation is responsible for providing specific written information, such as the purpose and recipient of the earmark, to the committee of jurisdiction. Further, Senate committees are responsible for compiling and presenting such information in accord with Senate rules. In the Senate, disclosure rules apply to any congressional earmark, limited tax benefit, or limited tariff benefit included in either the text of a bill or any report accompanying the measure, including a conference report and joint explanatory statement. The disclosure requirements apply to earmarks in appropriations legislation, authorizing legislation, and tax measures. Furthermore, they apply not only to measures reported by committees, but also to measures not reported by committees, floor amendments and conference reports.

Chapter 3- During 2007, both the House and Senate established new earmark transparency procedures for their separate chambers. They provide for public disclosure of approved earmarks and the identification of their congressional sponsors. In addition, they require disclosure of further information from each congressional sponsor, such as a certification that the sponsor has no financial interest in the earmark. Each House has also established procedures regarding new spending earmarks added to conference reports.

Chapter 4- On January 29, 2008, President George W. Bush signed Executive Order 13,457, "Protecting American Taxpayers from Government Spending on Wasteful Earmarks." The order states that it is the policy of the federal government "to be judicious in the expenditure of taxpayer dollars." In order "[t]o ensure the proper use of taxpayer funds," the order provides that the number and cost of earmarks should be reduced, that their origin and purposes should be transparent; and that they should be included in the text of bills voted upon by Congress and presented to the President. For appropriations laws and other legislation enacted after the date of the order, it directs executive agencies not to commit, obligate, or expend funds on the basis of earmarks included in any non-statutory source, including requests in reports of committees of Congress or other congressional documents or communications on behalf of Members of Congress, or any other non-statutory source, except when required by law or when an agency itself has determined that a project, program, grant, or other transaction has merit under statutory criteria or other merit-based decision-making.

Chapter 5- In 2007, both the House and the Senate established new earmark transparency procedures. They provide for public disclosure of approved earmarks and the identification of their congressional sponsors. These procedures currently are contained in House Rule XXI, clause 9, and Senate Rule XLIV. Under both chambers' rules, an earmark is a provision in legislation or report language that is included primarily at the request of a

Member, and provides, authorizes, or recommends a specific amount to an entity or to a specific state, locality, or congressional district.

Chapter 6- Earmarks—formally known as congressionally directed spending—have directed a significant amount of federal transportation spending in recent years. Proposals to ban earmarks in authorization and appropriations bills are under consideration in both houses of Congress. This report discusses how federal highway, transit, and aviation funding might be distributed under an earmark ban, and how members of Congress might influence the distribution.

In: Earmarks: Disclosure, Legal Developments... ISBN: 978-1-61324-588-0
Editors: Roger D. Halstead

Chapter 1

EARMARK DISCLOSURE RULES IN THE HOUSE: MEMBER AND COMMITTEE REQUIREMENTS

Megan Suzanne Lynch

SUMMARY

Earmark disclosure rules in both the House and Senate establish certain administrative responsibilities that vary by chamber. Under House rules, a Member requesting that an earmark be included in legislation is responsible for providing specific written information, such as the purpose and recipient of the earmark, to the committee of jurisdiction. Further, House committees are responsible for compiling, presenting, and maintaining such requests in accord with House rules. In the House, disclosure rules apply to any congressional earmark, limited tax benefit, or limited tariff benefit included in either the text of a bill or any report accompanying the measure, including a conference report and joint explanatory statement. The disclosure requirements apply to earmarks in appropriations legislation, authorizing legislation, and tax measures. Furthermore they apply not only to measures reported by committees, but also to measures not reported by committees, "manager's amendments," and conference reports.

INTRODUCTION

Earmark disclosure rules in both the House and Senate were implemented with the stated intention of bringing more transparency to congressionally directed spending. The administrative responsibilities associated with these rules vary by chamber. This report outlines the major administrative responsibilities of Members and committees of the House of Representatives associated with the chamber's earmark disclosure rules.[1]

HOUSE EARMARK DISCLOSURE RULE

House Rule XXI, clause 9, generally requires that certain types of measures be accompanied by a list of congressional earmarks, limited tax benefits or limited tariff benefits that are included in the measure or its report, or a statement that the proposition contains no earmarks. Depending upon the type of measure, the list or statement is to be included either in the measure's accompanying report, or printed in the *Congressional Record.*

Rule XXI, clause 9, explicitly defines congressional earmark, limited tax benefit, and limited tariff benefit as follows:

- **Congressional earmark**- a provision or report language included primarily at the request of a Member, Delegate, Resident Commissioner, or Senator providing, authorizing or recommending a specific amount of discretionary budget authority, credit authority, or other spending authority for a contract, loan, loan guarantee, grant, loan authority, or other expenditure with or to an entity, or targeted to a specific State, locality or congressional district, other than through a statutory or administrative formula driven or competitive award process.
- **Limited tax benefit**-(1) any revenue-losing provision that (A) provides a federal tax deduction, credit, exclusion, or preference to 10 or fewer beneficiaries under the Internal Revenue Code of 1986, and (B) contains eligibility criteria that are not uniform in application with respect to potential beneficiaries of such provision; or (2) any federal tax provision which provides one beneficiary temporary or permanent transition relief from a change to the Internal Revenue Code of 1986.

- **Limited tariff benefit**- a provision modifying the Harmonized Tariff Schedule of the United States in a manner that benefits 10 or fewer entities.

If either the list of earmarks[2] or the letter stating that no earmark exists in the measure is absent, a point of order may lie against the measure's floor consideration. The point of order applies only in the absence of such a list or letter, and does not speak to the completeness or the accuracy of either document.[3] A point of order may lie against the consideration of any general appropriations conference report containing earmarks that are included in conference reports but not committed to conference by either House and not in a House or Senate committee report on the legislation. Such a point of order would be disposed of by a question of consideration, debatable for 20 minutes.[4]

LEGISLATION SUBJECT TO THE RULE

House earmark disclosure rules apply to any congressional earmark included in either the text of the bill or the committee report accompanying the bill, as well as the conference report and joint explanatory statement. The disclosure requirements apply to items in authorizing legislation, appropriations legislation, and tax measures. Furthermore, they apply not only to measures reported by committees, but also to unreported measures, "manager's amendments,"[5] Senate bills and conference reports.

These earmark disclosure requirements, however, do not apply to all legislation at all times. For example, when a measure is considered, under the "suspension of the rules" procedure, House rules are laid aside, and therefore earmark disclosure rules do not apply. Also not subject to the rule are floor amendments (except a "manager's amendment"), amendments between the houses, or amendments considered as adopted under a self-executing special rule, including a committee amendment in the nature of a substitute made in order as original text.[6]

REQUIREMENTS FOR MEMBERS SUBMITTING EARMARK REQUESTS

Under House Rule XXIII, clause 17(a), Members[7] requesting a congressional earmark are required to provide a written statement to the chairman and ranking minority member of the committee of jurisdiction that includes

1. the Member's name;
2. the name and address of the intended earmark recipient (if there is no specific recipient, the location of the intended activity should be included);
3. in the case of a limited tax or tariff benefit, identification of the individual or entities reasonably anticipated to benefit, to the extent known to the Member;
4. the purpose of the earmark; and
5. a certification that the Member or Member's spouse has no financial interest in such an earmark. [8]

When submitting earmark requests, it is important to note that individual committees and subcommittees often have their own additional administrative requirements beyond those required by House rules (e.g., prioritizing requests or submitting request forms online). The House Appropriations Committee, for example, has stated that it will require Members requesting earmarks to post information regarding their earmark requests on their personal website. This information must be posted at the time of the request and must include the purpose of the earmark and why it is a valuable use of taxpayer funds. [9] Additionally, the House Appropriations Committee has announced that they will no longer approve requests for earmarks that are directed to for-profit entities.[10]

Committees may also establish relevant policy requirements (e.g., requiring matching funds for earmark requests) or restrictions regarding earmark requests (e.g., not considering earmark requests for certain appropriations accounts or disallowing multi-year funding requests). In addition, committees and subcommittees often have deadlines, especially for earmark requests in appropriations legislation. For this reason, it is important to check with individual committees and subcommittees to learn of any supplemental earmark request requirements or restrictions.[11]

The committee of jurisdiction is responsible for identifying earmarks in both the legislative text and any accompanying reports. When it is not clear whether a Member request constitutes an earmark, the committee of jurisdiction may be able to provide guidance.

When submitting an earmark request, it may be relevant whether the Member wants the earmark to be included in the text of the bill or the committee report accompanying the bill. Committees may make an administrative distinction between these two categories in terms of the submission of earmark requests, and there may be policy implications of an earmark's placement in either the bill text or the committee report. For example, under Executive Order 13,457[12] issued in January 2008, executive agencies are directed not to commit, obligate, or expend funds that were the result of an earmark included in non-statutory language, such as a committee report.[13]

REQUIREMENTS FOR COMMITTEES

Under House rules, earmark disclosure responsibilities of House committees and conference committees fall into three major categories: (1) determining if a spending provision is an earmark; (2) compiling earmark requests for presentation to the full chamber; and (3) preserving the earmark requests. Individual committees may establish their own additional requirements.

Committees of jurisdiction must use their discretion to decide what constitutes an earmark. Definitions in House rules, as well as past earmark designations during the 110th Congress, may provide guidance in determining if a certain provision constitutes an earmark.

House Rule XXIII, clause 17(b) states that in the case of any reported bill or conference report, a list of included earmarks and their sponsors, or a statement declaring the absence of earmarks, must be included in the corresponding committee report or joint explanatory statement. In the case of a measure not reported by a committee, or a "manager's amendment," the committee of initial referral must cause a list of earmarks and their sponsors, or letter stating the absence of earmarks, to be printed in the *Congressional Record* before floor consideration is in order. The House Appropriations Committee has stated that it will make earmark disclosure tables publically available the same day that a subcommittee reports their bill.[14]

A conference report to accompany a regular appropriations bill must identify congressional earmarks in the conference report or joint explanatory statement that were not specified in the legislation or report as it initially passed either chamber.[15]

Each House committee and conference committee is responsible for "maintaining" all written requests for earmarks received, even those not ultimately included in the measure or the measure's report. Furthermore, those requests which were included in any measure reported by the committee must not only be "maintained," but must also be "open for public inspection." Rule XXIII does not specify how the information shall be "maintained" and "open for public inspection."

End Notes

[1] This report outlines the administrative responsibilities relating to earmark disclosure contained in House rules. It does not discuss earmark-related responsibilities required by either party's conference or caucus, or those that may be adopted by individual committees. For information regarding administrative duties associated with Senate earmark disclosure rules, see CRS Report RS22867, *Earmark Disclosure Rules in the Senate: Member and Committee Requirements*, by Megan Suzanne Lynch. For further information on the rules governing congressional earmarks, see CRS Report RL34462, *House and Senate Procedural Rules Concerning Earmark Disclosure*, by Sandy Streeter.

[2] For the purposes of this report, from this point forward the term "earmark" includes any congressional earmark, limited tax benefit or limited tariff benefit.

[3] U.S. Congress, House, *Constitution, Jefferson's Manual, and Rules of the House of Representatives of the United States, 110th Congress*, H. Doc 109-157 (Washington: GPO, 2007), § 1068e.

[4] House Rule XXI, 9(c), adopted under H.Res. 5 (111th Congress), January 6, 2009. This provision had previously been adopted as a standing order of the House under H.Res. 491 (110th Congress).

[5] As defined in the rule, and clarified in a letter from the House Parliamentarian to the Chairman of the House Committee on Rules *(Congressional Record*, daily edition, vol. 153, October 3, 2007, pp. H1 1184-H111 85.) a "manager's amendment" is "an amendment offered at the outset of consideration for amendment by a member of a committee of initial referral under the terms of a special rule."

[6] Ibid.

[7] In this report, "Member" includes Members, Delegates or the Resident Commissioner.

[8] Guidance and clarification in determining a financial interest is available in U.S. Congress, House Committee on Standards of Official Conduct, *The House Ethics Manual*, 110th Cong., 2nd sess., 2008, (Washington: GPO, 2008), pp. 238-239. Available also at http://ethics

[9] As stated in the January 6, 2009 joint press release from the House and Senate Appropriations Committees Chairmen titled, *House and Senate Appropriations Committees Announce Additional Reforms in Committee Earmark Policy*, available at http://appropriations

[10] As stated in the March 10, 2010 press release from the House Appropriations Committee Chairman titled, *Appropriations Committees Bans For-Profit Earmarks*, available at http://appropriations 2010_Earmark_Reforms_Release-3. 10.20 10.pdf.

[11] Often these requirements are communicated through a "Dear Colleague" letter or through the committee's website.

[12] "Protecting American Taxpayers From Governmental Spending on Wasteful Earmarks," Executive Order 13,457, January 29, 2008, available at http://www.whitehouse.gov/news/releases/2008/01/20080129-5.html.

[13] For further information, see CRS Report RL34373, *Earmarks Executive Order: Legal Issues*, by Thomas J. Nicola and T. J. Halstead.

[14] As stated in the January 6, 2009 joint press release.

[15] During the 110th Congress, it was the practice to include such earmarks in the list required by Rule XXI, clause 9, and identify them with an asterisk. Note that the Senate defines items related to earmark disclosure somewhat differently, for more information, see CRS Report RS22867, *Earmark Disclosure Rules in the Senate: Member and Committee Requirements*, by Megan Suzanne Lynch.

In: Earmarks: Disclosure, Legal Developments… ISBN: 978-1-61324-588-0
Editors: Roger D. Halstead

Chapter 2

EARMARK DISCLOSURE RULES IN THE SENATE: MEMBER AND COMMITTEE REQUIREMENTS

Megan Suzanne Lynch

SUMMARY

Earmark disclosure rules in both the House and Senate establish certain administrative responsibilities that vary by chamber. Under Senate rules, a Senator requesting that an earmark be included in legislation is responsible for providing specific written information, such as the purpose and recipient of the earmark, to the committee of jurisdiction. Further, Senate committees are responsible for compiling and presenting such information in accord with Senate rules. In the Senate, disclosure rules apply to any congressional earmark, limited tax benefit, or limited tariff benefit included in either the text of a bill or any report accompanying the measure, including a conference report and joint explanatory statement. The disclosure requirements apply to earmarks in appropriations legislation, authorizing legislation, and tax measures. Furthermore, they apply not only to measures reported by committees, but also to measures not reported by committees, floor amendments and conference reports.

INTRODUCTION

Earmark[1] disclosure rules in both the House and Senate were implemented with the stated intention of bringing more transparency to congressionally-directed spending. The administrative responsibilities associated with these new rules vary by chamber. This report outlines the major administrative responsibilities of Senators and committees of the Senate associated with the chamber's earmark disclosure rules.[2]

SENATE EARMARK DISCLOSURE RULE

Senate Rule XLIV[3] prohibits a vote on a motion to proceed to consider a measure or a vote on adoption of a conference report, unless the chair of the committee or the Majority Leader (or designee) certifies that a complete list of earmarks and the name of each Senator requesting each earmark is available on a publicly accessible congressional website in a searchable form at least 48 hours before the vote. If a Senator proposes a floor amendment containing an additional earmark,[4] those items must be printed in the *Congressional Record* as soon as "practicable."[5]

Rule XLIV, paragraph 5, explicitly defines congressionally directed spending item, limited tax benefit, and limited tariff benefit as follows:

- **Congressionally directed spending item**- a provision or report language included primarily at the request of a Senator providing, authorizing or recommending a specific amount of discretionary budget authority, credit authority, or other spending authority for a contract, loan, loan guarantee, grant, loan authority, or other expenditure with or to an entity, or targeted to a specific State, locality or congressional district, other than through a statutory or administrative formula driven or competitive award process.
- **Limited tax benefit**- any revenue provision that (A) provides a federal tax deduction, credit, exclusion, or preference to a particular beneficiary or limited group of beneficiaries under the Internal Revenue Code of 1986, and (B) contains eligibility criteria that are not uniform in application with respect to potential beneficiaries of such provision.

- **Limited tariff benefit**- a provision modifying the Harmonized Tariff Schedule of the United States in a manner that benefits 10 or fewer entities.

If the earmark certification requirements have not been met, a point of order may lie against consideration of the measure or vote on the conference report. A point of order would not apply to floor amendments.

LEGISLATION SUBJECT TO THE RULE

Senate earmark disclosure rules apply to any congressional earmark included in either the text of the bill or the committee report accompanying the bill, as well as the conference report and joint explanatory statement. The disclosure requirements apply to items in authorizing legislation, appropriations legislation, and tax measures. Furthermore, they apply not only to measures reported by committees, but also to unreported measures, amendments, House bills, and conference reports.

REQUIREMENTS FOR SENATORS SUBMITTING EARMARK REQUESTS

Under Senate Rule XLIV, paragraph 6, a Senator requesting that a congressional earmark be included in a measure is required to provide a written statement to the chair and ranking minority member of the committee of jurisdiction that includes

1. the Senator's name;
2. the name and address of the intended earmark recipient (if there is no specific recipient, the location of the intended activity should be included);
3. in the case of a limited tax or tariff benefit, identification of the individual or entities reasonably anticipated to benefit, to the extent known to the Senator;
4. the purpose of the earmark; and
5. a certification that neither the Senator or Senator's immediate family has a financial interest in such an earmark.[6]

When submitting earmark requests, it is important to note that individual committees and subcommittees often have their own additional administrative requirements beyond those required by Senate rules (e.g., prioritizing requests or submitting request forms electronically). The Senate Appropriations Committee, for example, has stated that it will require Members requesting earmarks to post information regarding their earmark requests on their personal website. This information must be posted at the time of the request and must include the purpose of the earmark and why it is a valuable use of taxpayer funds.[7]

They may also establish relevant policy requirements (e.g., requiring matching funds for earmark requests) or restrictions (e.g., not considering earmark requests for certain appropriations accounts or disallowing multi-year funding requests). In addition, committees and subcommittees often have deadlines, especially for earmark requests in appropriations legislation. For this reason, it is important to check with individual committees and subcommittees to learn of any supplemental earmark request requirements or restrictions.[8]

The committee of jurisdiction is responsible for identifying earmarks in the legislative text and any accompanying reports. Therefore, when it is not clear whether a Senatorial request constitutes an earmark, the committee of jurisdiction may be able to provide guidance.

When submitting an earmark request, it may be relevant whether the Senator wants the earmark to be included in the text of the bill or the committee report accompanying the bill. Committees may make an administrative distinction between these two categories in terms of the submission of earmark requests, and there may be policy implications of an earmark's placement in either the bill text or the committee report. For example, under Executive Order 13,457[9] issued in January 2008, executive agencies are directed not to commit, obligate, or expend funds that were the result of an earmark included in non-statutory language, such as a committee report.[10]

If during consideration of a measure, a Senator proposes an amendment[11] that contains an additional earmark[12], the Senator shall ensure that a list of earmarks (and the name of any Senator who submitted a request to the Senator for each item included) is printed in the *Congressional Record* as soon as "practicable."

Requirements for Committees

Under the Senate rule, earmark disclosure responsibilities of Senate committees and conference committees fall into three major categories: (1) determining if a spending provision is an earmark; (2) compiling earmark requests for presentation,[13] and (3) certifying that requirements under Rule XLIV have been met.

Committees of jurisdiction may use their discretion to decide what constitutes an earmark. Definitions in Senate rules, as well as past earmark designations during the 110th Congress, may provide guidance in determining if a certain provision constitutes an earmark.

U.S. SENATE, COMMITTEE ON AGRICULTURE, NUTRITION, AND FORESTRY,
Washington, DC, November 5, 2007.

I certify that the information required by Senate Rule XLIV, related to congressionally directed spending in S. 2302 has been available on a publicly accessible website in a searchable format for at least 48 hours before a vote on the pending bill.

TOM HARKIN,
Chairman.

Source: *Congressional Record*, daily edition, vol. 153, November 5, 2007, p. S13751.

Senate Rule XLIV states that before consideration is in order on a measure or conference report, a list of included earmarks and their sponsors must be identified through lists, charts, or some means, and made available on a publicly accessible congressional website for at least 48 hours.[14] The Senate Appropriations Committee has stated that it will make earmark disclosure tables publically available the same day that a subcommittee reports the bill.[15] In the case of measures, the list of earmarks (and Senate sponsors) on the congressional website must be "searchable." Lists associated with conference reports should also be in a searchable format, but only to the extent technically feasible. Senate rules state that a committee report containing a list of earmarks (and their sponsors) that is available online satisfies the disclosure requirement. The rule also requires the applicable committee to make the certifications of no financial interest available online. The rule does not specify how long after consideration any of these required materials must be maintained.

The rule states that consideration of a measure or conference report is not in order until the applicable committee chair or the Majority Leader (or designee) "certifies" that the requirements stated above have been met. While the rule does not state what constitutes certification, it has been the practice of the committee chair to make a statement on the Senate floor, or submit a written statement to be printed in the *Congressional Record,* confirming compliance with Rule XLIV's disclosure requirements. An example of a certification letter is provided below.

End Notes

[1] In Senate rules, the term "congressionally directed spending item" is used in place of earmark. For the purposes of this report, the terms will be used interchangeably. From this point forward, the term "earmark" refers to any congressionally directed spending item, limited tax benefit, or limited tariff benefit.

[2] This report outlines the administrative responsibilities relating to earmark disclosure contained in Senate rules. It does not discuss earmark-related responsibilities required by either party's conference or caucus, or those that may be adopted by individual committees. For information regarding administrative duties associated with House earmark disclosure rules, see CRS Report RS22866, *Earmark Disclosure Rules in the House: Member and Committee Requirements*, by Megan Suzanne Lynch. For further information on the rules governing congressional earmarks, see CRS Report RL34462, *House and Senate Procedural Rules Concerning Earmark Disclosure*, by Sandy Streeter.

[3] The Senate included this rule in the Honest Leadership and Open Government Act of 2007, which became law on September 14, 2007. (Section 521 of P.L. 110-81, 121 Stat.760)

[4] The rule does not apply to all earmarks in floor amendments, only those "not included in the bill or joint resolution as placed on the calendar or as reported by any committee, in a committee report on such a bill or joint resolution, or a committee report of the Senate on a companion measure," as stated in Rule XLIV, paragraph 4(a).

[5] The rule does not define the term "practicable."

[6] For more information on the definition of "immediate family" see *Definition of "Immediate Family" for Requested Appropriations,* released by the Senate Select Committee on Ethics, September 12, 2007, available at http://www.ethics.

[7] As stated in the January 6, 2009 joint press release from the House and Senate Appropriations Committees Chairmen titled, *House and Senate Appropriations Committees Announce Additional Reforms in Committee Earmark Policy*, available at http://appropriations

[8] Often these requirements are communicated through a "Dear Colleague" letter, committee staff memos or through the committee's website.

[9] "Protecting American Taxpayers From Governmental Spending on Wasteful Earmarks," Executive Order 13,457, January 29, 2008, available at http://www.whitehouse.gov/news/releases/2008/01/20080129-5.html.

[10] For further information, see CRS Report RL34373, *Earmarks Executive Order: Legal Issues*, by Thomas J. Nicola and T. J. Halstead.

[11] Including amendments in the nature of a substitute.

[12] The rule does not apply to all earmarks in floor amendments, only those "not included in the bill or joint resolution as placed on the calendar or as reported by any committee, in a committee report on such a bill or joint resolution, or a committee report of the Senate on a companion measure," as stated in Rule XLIV, paragraph 4(a).

[13] In the case of an earmark in any classified portion of a report accompanying a measure, Paragraph 7 Senate Rule XLIV states that the committee of jurisdiction should, to the greatest extent practicable, consistent with the need to protect national security, including intelligence sources and methods, include an unclassified program description, funding level and name of the Senate sponsor.

[14] Rule XLIV, paragraph 4(b) states that when a committee reports a measure, the earmark list should be made available online in a searchable format as soon as "practicable." The rule does not define "practicable."

[15] In the case that the appropriations legislation has not been marked up by a subcommittee, the Senate Appropriations Committee will make earmark disclosure tables publically available 24 hours before full Committee consideration of the bill. As stated in the January 6, 2009 joint press release.

In: Earmarks: Disclosure, Legal Developments... ISBN: 978-1-61324-588-0
Editors: Roger D. Halstead

Chapter 3

HOUSE AND SENATE PROCEDURAL RULES CONCERNING EARMARK DISCLOSURE

Sandy Streeter

SUMMARY

During 2007, both the House and Senate established new earmark transparency procedures for their separate chambers. They provide for public disclosure of approved earmarks and the identification of their congressional sponsors. In addition, they require disclosure of further information from each congressional sponsor, such as a certification that the sponsor has no financial interest in the earmark. Each House has also established procedures regarding new spending earmarks added to conference reports.

The House originally established its procedures through adoption of two House resolutions. On January 5, 2007, the House completed action on H.Res. 6 (110th Congress), adopting the 110th Congress rules package, including new provisions in House Rule XXI to require public disclosure of approved earmarks, their sponsors, and the additional information. On June 18, 2007, the House adopted a standing order, H.Res. 491 (110th Congress), to require transparency for new spending earmarks added to conference reports on the 12 annual regular appropriations bills. On January 6, 2009, the House adopted the rules package for the 111th Congress, H.Res. 5 (111th Congress), which incorporated the provisions of H.Res. 491 into House Rule XXI, clause 9.

In the Senate, Rule XLIV was adopted through the Honest Leadership and Open Government Act of 2007 (P.L. 110-81), which became law on September 14, 2007. The new rule provides for public disclosure of each "congressionally directed spending item," its sponsors, and "no financial interest" certifications. It also includes a procedure to strike certain new items of spending added to conference reports.

The House rule generally prohibits consideration of a measure, manager's amendment, or conference report unless a list of earmarks and the name of each sponsoring Member (or a statement that there are no earmarks) is available before consideration. The Senate rule prohibits a vote on a motion to proceed to consider a measure or a vote on adoption of a conference report, unless the chair of the committee or Majority Leader certifies that a complete list of earmarks and the name of each Senator requesting each earmark is available on a publicly accessible congressional website 48 hours before the vote.

Both House and Senate rules require earmark sponsors to provide similar information on each earmark to the committee of jurisdiction, but these rules include different public disclosure requirements regarding the information. Neither requirement is enforced by points of order. In the House, the applicable committee is to make "open to public inspection" the Member's entire written statement on certain approved earmarks. The Senate rule requires the applicable committee to make available on the Internet the certifications of no financial interest.

With regard to certain spending earmarks first specified in conference, the House requires public disclosure of those earmarks and the names of those Members that requested each earmark identified. The Senate rule provides a procedure to strike certain new items of spending, including earmarks, from a conference report.

INTRODUCTION

During 2007, both the House and Senate established new earmark transparency procedures for their separate chambers. They provide for public disclosure of approved earmarks and the identification of their congressional sponsors.[1] In addition, they require disclosure of further information from each congressional sponsor, such as a certification that the sponsor has no financial interest in the earmark. Each House has also established procedures regarding new spending earmarks added to conference reports.

The House originally established its procedures through adoption of two House resolutions. On January 5, 2007, the House completed action on H.Res. 6 (110th Congress), adopting the 110th Congress rules package, including new provisions in House Rule XXI to require public disclosure of approved earmarks, their sponsors, and the additional information.[2] On June 18, 2007, the House adopted a standing order, H.Res. 491 (110th Congress), to require transparency for new spending earmarks added to conference reports on the 12 annual regular appropriations bills. On January 6, 2009, the House adopted the rules package for the 111th Congress, H.Res. 5 (111th Congress), which incorporated the provisions of H.Res. 491 into House Rule XXI, clause 9.[3]

In the Senate, Rule XLIV was adopted through the Honest Leadership and Open Government Act of 2007 (P.L. 110-81),[4] which became law on September 14, 2007. The new rule provides for public disclosure of each "congressionally directed spending item," its sponsors, and "no financial interest" certifications. It also includes a procedure to strike certain new items of spending added to conference reports.

This report describes and compares the procedures and requirements in House and Senate rules, including the House requirement regarding the use of earmarks as leverage for votes. In addition, individual House and Senate committees may have additional requirements for earmarks submitted for their consideration, but these are not covered in this report.[5]

When submitting an earmark request, there may also be other considerations relevant to the individual Member's request, such as whether the earmark should be included in the text of the bill or the committee report accompanying the bill. Committees may make an administrative distinction between these two categories in terms of the submission of earmark requests, and there may be policy implications of an earmark's placement in either the bill text or the committee report as well.[6]

EARMARK DEFINITION

For purposes of the procedures discussed below, both House and Senate rules[7] provide definitions for spending earmarks, limited tax benefits, and limited tariff benefits.

Spending Earmark Definition

The spending earmark definitions in House Rule XXI, clause 9, and Senate Rule XLIV are identical, except the identification of earmark requesters.

For purposes of all the disclosure requirements above, a spending earmark is a provision in legislation or report language[8] that meets specific criteria. First, the provision or language is primarily included at the request of a Representative, Delegate, the Resident Commissioner, or Senator under the House rule (or a Senator under the Senate rule). Second, the provision or language provides, authorizes, or recommends a specific amount of discretionary budget authority, credit authority, or other spending authority for certain purposes (1) with or to an entity,[9] or (2) targeted to a specific state, locality, or congressional district. The purposes are a contract, grant, loan, loan guarantee, loan authority, or other expenditure. Finally, any of the above spending set asides that are selected through a statutory or administrative formula-driven or competitive-award process are excluded.

The definition is broad. It includes earmarks funded or recommended in appropriations legislation, as well as other non-appropriations legislation (such as authorizations), conference reports, and accompanying report language.

Limited Tariff Benefit Definition

The definitions in the House and Senate rules are identical. Such tariff benefits are defined as "a provision modifying the Harmonized Tariff Schedule of the United States in a manner that benefits 10 or fewer entities." This definition targets provisions in "miscellaneous duty suspension bills" or "miscellaneous tariff bills" (MTBs), which seek to temporarily reduce or eliminate tariffs on imports of particular commodities. The vast majority of tariff suspensions are on chemicals, raw materials, or other components used in the manufacturing process.[10]

Limited Tax Benefit Definition

In contrast to the previous definitions, the House and Senate definitions of limited tax benefits are somewhat different. Under the Senate rule a *limited tax benefit* is defined as a revenue provision that provides a tax deduction, credit, exclusion, or preference to a particular beneficiary or limited group of beneficiaries under the tax code and contains eligibility criteria that are not uniform in application with respect to potential beneficiaries of the provision.

The House rule is more specific, and uses the term *limited tax benefit* to apply to (1) a revenue- losing provision that provides a tax deduction, credit, exclusion, or preference to no more than 10 beneficiaries under the tax code and contains eligibility criteria that are not uniform in application with respect to potential beneficiaries of the provision; or (2) a tax provision that provides one beneficiary with transitional relief from a change to the tax code.

PUBLIC DISCLOSURE PROCEDURES ON EARMARK REQUESTS

Earmark List and Congressional Earmark Sponsors

The rules in both the House and Senate include parliamentary procedures regarding greater transparency of congressional sponsors of earmarks.

House Rule XXI, clause 9

This rule prohibits House consideration of legislation, certain amendments, or conference reports, unless either

- a list of earmarks in such legislation, amendment, conference report, or any accompanying report language and the name of any House Member[11] who requested an earmark(s) on the list is made available; or
- a statement that there are no earmarks is made available.

Only selected amendments to legislative measures are covered under this rule: amendments in committee-reported legislation and manager's amendments. A *manager's amendment* is an amendment offered at the outset of consideration for amendment by a member of a committee of initial referral, under the terms of a special rule. [12] Major legislation is typically brought up on the House floor by a special rule, which provides the terms for consideration of the measure, and may also limit consideration of floor amendments, specify the order for consideration of specific amendments, or waive various House rules. After the House adopts a special rule, by a majority vote, Members consider the measure on the House floor. House Rule XXI, clause 9, does not cover certain forms of amendments,[13] such as an amendment between the Houses,[14] an amendment automatically agreed to upon adoption of a special rule, an amendment offered during floor consideration, or a committee amendment in the nature of a substitute made in order as original text for purposes of amendment.[15]

Under the House rule, the required list of earmarks (and congressional sponsors) or statement that there are no earmarks must be disclosed in specified public documents. For committee-reported legislation and conference reports, either a list or statement must be included in the applicable report language. Regarding non-reported legislation, the chair of each committee of initial referral is required to have a list or a statement printed in the *Congressional Record* prior to consideration of the legislation. The proponent of a manager's amendment must also have a list or statement printed in the *Congressional Record* prior to consideration of the amendment.

While the House has established rules designed to provide time for Members to review the contents of committee reports, conference reports, and joint explanatory statements before floor consideration, the House may waive these requirements. In cases in which a committee provides time for review, Members have an opportunity, for example, to draft amendments striking specific earmarks in a reported bill or lobby against a conference report. Under House Rule XIII, clause 4(a), committee-reported legislation may not generally be considered on the House floor until the accompanying committee report has been available to Members for at least three calendar days.[16]

House Rule XXII, clause 8(a), provides a similar three-day availability requirement for conference reports. The conference report and attached joint explanatory statement must be available in the *Congressional Record* for at least three calendar days prior to consideration, and copies of the conference report and joint explanatory statement must be available for at least two hours before consideration.[17] The House, however, typically adopts special rules providing for consideration of conference reports that waive all points of order, including these.

The earmark and sponsor disclosure requirements are not self-enforcing; a Member must raise a point of order on the House floor against consideration of the legislation, amendment, or conference report.

A point of order raised under this subsection may be based only on the failure to include a list of earmarks (and sponsors) or a statement that there are no earmarks in the report language or *Congressional Record*, as applicable.[18]

In response to a parliamentary inquiry, the Speaker pro tempore explained that the rule

> ... does not contemplate a question of order relating to the content of the statement offered in compliance with the rule. Argument concerning the adequacy of the list or the probity of a disclaimer is a matter that may be addressed by debate on the merits of the measure or by other means collateral to the review of the chair.[19]

Each committee, therefore, is left solely responsible for determining the contents of the list.

The House rule prohibits House consideration of a special rule that waives the public disclosure requirements, and includes a special procedure to implement this prohibition. If a Member raises a point of order against considering a special rule that includes such a waiver, the presidingofficer does not rule on the point of order. Instead the House decides, by majority vote, whether to consider the special rule.[20] The House rule provides 20 minutes of debate, equally divided and controlled by the initiator of the point of order and an opponent. No other intervening motion is allowed, except one that the House adjourn. This procedure effectively allows the House to decide by a separate vote whether to allow this public disclosure requirement to be waived.[21]

Senate Rule XLIV

This rule provides different procedures from the House, but it is also intended to improve public disclosure of earmarks including the name of each Senator who requested any identified earmark. Senate Rule XLIV prohibits a vote on a motion to proceed to consider any committee-reported legislative measure (and any amendment included in the text of the reported bill) or non-reported Senate legislative measure, unless the chair of the applicable committee or the Majority Leader (or designee) provides certain certifications.[22] Similarly, the Senate can not vote on adoption of a conference report unless the chair or Majority Leader (or designee) makes a similar certification.

The chair or Majority Leader must certify that a list (or a chart or other similar form) of all earmarks (including those in the applicable measure, conference report, or accompanying report language, if any) and the name of each Senator who submitted a request for each item listed has been available on a publicly accessible congressional website for at least 48 hours before such vote.[23] In the case of measures, they must also certify that the list of earmarks (and Senate sponsors) on the congressional website are in a searchable format. Lists associated with conference reports should also be in a searchable format, but only to the extent technically feasible.

If the presiding officer sustains a point of order against a vote on a motion to proceed, consideration on the motion is suspended until a certification is made and the sponsor (or designee) of the motion requests consideration to resume. Under Rule XLIV, paragraph 3, if a point of order is sustained against a conference report, it would be set aside.

These rules are not self-enforcing; a Senator must raise a point of order against the vote.[24]

Senate Rule XLIV provides two procedures to waive these requirements and restricts appeals of the presiding officer's rulings on such points of order. Unlike the House, the Senate does not have a generally applicable mechanism to waive its rules. Although a waiver motion is available for points of order under the Budget Act and similar requirements, the Senate standing rules must typically be waived by unanimous consent (that is, no Senator objects to a unanimous consent request to waive a rule).[25] Senate Rule XLIV, however, incorporates a waiver motion similar to that used under the Budget Act, and allows any Senator to make a motion to waive any of these points of order. An affirmative vote of three-fifths of all Senators (60, if there are no vacancies) is required to adopt the motion. Senators may debate the motion for up to one hour, with the time equally divided and controlled by the Majority and Minority Leaders (or their designees). These points of order may also be waived if the Majority and Minority Leaders jointly agree that "such a waiver is necessary as a result of a significant disruption to Senate facilities or to the availability of the Internet."[26]

The Senate rule places restrictions on consideration of appeals of the chair's rulings on these points of order. Any Senator may appeal the presiding officer's ruling on most Senate rules. Such appeals are generally debatable, and debate may be ended by cloture (requiring three-fifths vote of all Senators to adopt the cloture motion) or by a motion to table, which would uphold the chair's ruling. The appeal procedure included in Rule XLIV allows only one appeal and limits debate to one hour.

Amendments in the reported bill or offered from the floor that include earmarks are covered under the rule, but the procedures differ. Those amendments in the text of the reported bill are subject to the same point of order described above that applies to reported measures. Regarding amendments offered from the floor, the rule recommends that the sponsor of an amendment that includes an additional earmark[27] ensure, as soon as practicable, that (1) a list of each earmark and (2) the name of any Senator requesting each earmark on the list be printed in the *Congressional Record*. This includes full-substitute amendments offered from the floor. As in the House, amendments between the Houses are not covered under this rule.

Specified Information (Including Certifications) from Congressional Earmark Sponsors

Both House and Senate rules[28] require earmark sponsors to provide similar information on each earmark to the committee of jurisdiction, but these rules include different public disclosure requirements regarding the information. Neither requirement is enforced by points of order.

These rules require each Member requesting an earmark in legislation (conference report or accompanying report language) to submit specific written information to the chair and ranking member of the committee of jurisdiction. Each sponsor shall submit in writing (1) the sponsor's name; (2) in the case of a spending earmark, the name and address of the intended recipient[29] or, if there is no specifically intended recipient, the intended location of the activity; (3) in the case of a limited tax or tariff benefit, the sponsor must identify the individual or entities reasonably anticipated to benefit, to the extent known by the sponsor; (4) the purpose of the earmark; and (5) a certification of no pecuniary interest in such earmark.

While the House rule requires a certification that neither the Member nor the Member's spouse have any financial interest in the earmark, the Senate rule requires a certification that neither the Senator nor the Senator's immediate family have any pecuniary interest, consistent with paragraph 9 of the rule.[30]

Regarding the differing House and Senate public availability requirements, in the House, the applicable committee is to make "open to public inspection" the Member's written statement on any earmark included in a measure or conference report. Each House committee has the discretion to determine its own public disclosure procedures. The Senate rule, on the other hand, recommends that each committee make available only the certification of "no pecuniary interest" for each earmark included in a Senate measure reported or considered by the Senate, conference report, or report language, if any. In addition, under the Senate rule, committees are to make the certifications available for public inspection on the Internet, as soon as practicable.

Classified Earmarks

The Senate rule specifically recommends that the committees of jurisdiction include on these lists applicable classified spending earmarks to the greatest extent practicable, consistent with the need to protect national security (including intelligence sources and methods). The information for each earmark identified should include an unclassified program description, spending amount, and name of Senate sponsor. The House rule does not include a specific provision on classified earmarks. Public disclosure of these earmarks and their sponsors are made under the disclosure requirements as discussed above.

CONFERENCE REPORT PROCEDURES AFFECTING NEW EARMARKS

House Rule XXI, clause 9(b), and Senate Rule XLIV, paragraph 8, both address certain spending earmarks, sometimes referred to as "air-drops," added in a conference report (and joint explanatory statement under the House rule) that were not specified in the House- or Senate- passed versions of the applicable bill (or in the accompanying House or Senate committee reports in the House rule). The House rule provides a public disclosure requirement for such earmark add-ons similar to the transparency requirement affecting earmarks, in general, associated with conference reports discussed above (see "House Rule XXI, clause 9" section). The Senate rule, by contrast, provides a procedure to strike certain spending add-ons, including applicable spending earmarks.

House Rule XXI, Clause 9(b)

This rule highlights new earmarks added in conference by requiring a list and congressional sponsors. It prohibits House consideration of a conference report to a regular appropriations bills,[31] unless either

- a list of new earmarks added to the conference report or joint explanatory statement and the name of any Member[32] who requested an earmark(s) on the list is included in the joint explanatory statement; or
- a statement that there are no earmarks is made available.

In response to the original version of this rule (H.Res. 491, 110th Congress), the House Appropriations Committee has generally been identifying earmark add-ons in the required list of general earmarks (and sponsors) associated with conference reports to regular appropriations bills.

Clause 9(b) provides two major differences to the procedure requiring a list of earmarks, in general, and congressional earmark sponsors associated with conference reports discussed above, under the "House Rule XXI, clause 9" section. First, the "airdropped-earmark" requirement only applies to conference reports to the 12 annual regular appropriations bills, instead of all spending measures as well as tariff and revenue measures. Second, upon a point of order, the House decides, by majority vote, whether to consider the conference report with "airdropped" earmarks; as opposed to a ruling by the chair. The House decides to consider such a conference report by the same procedures the House decides to consider a special rule waiving these points of order:[33] up to a 20-minute debate, equally divided and controlled (see above, "House Rule XXI, clause 9" section). Due to this provision, the House can debate and vote on whether to consider a conference report (or special rule waiving this requirement) even when the clause 9(b) may not have been violated.

Senate Rule XLIV, Paragraph 8

The Senate rule establishes a new procedure to strike certain new spending earmarks, as well as other spending, added to conference reports.[34] It applies to provisions providing funds (both discretionary and direct (or mandatory) spending), but not provisions authorizing or reauthorizing funds. The rule also does not apply to limited tax or tariff benefits added in conference.

The provision in Senate Rule XLIV concerning conference is not directed against congressionally directed spending items, as are the provisions concerning disclosure described above, but instead allows any Senator to raise a point of order against any provision or provisions in a conference report that contain a specific spending level for a specific program, project, activity, or account when no specific funding level was provided for the applicable item in the House- or Senate- passed versions of the measure. The Presiding Officer may sustain points of order against one or more provisions in the conference report. This rule does not apply to language in joint explanatory statements, only those provisions in the legislative text of conference reports.

The rule supplements Senate Rule XXVIII, which generally prohibits conferees from including in a conference report a new matter not dealt with in either the House- or Senate-passed versions of a measure. Under current Senate practice and precedents, however, earmarks air-dropped into conference reports are not typically interpreted as new matter. Rule XXVIII provides that in cases in which one of the versions of the bill is an amendment in the nature of a substitute, which is typically the case, the conferees may include a germane modification of the subjects in disagreement. Under existing precedents, earmarks added to a conference report are often considered germane modifications. For example, regular appropriations measures provide funding to each department and large independent agency by distributing the spending among several accounts.[35] Funding levels for programs, projects, or activities within an account, such as most earmarks included in legislative text, are generally considered germane modifications.

A Senator may raise a point of order under Rule XLIV against any provision or provisions in a conference report that contain a specific spending level for a specific program, project, activity, or account when no specific funding level was provided for the applicable item in the House- or Senate-passed versions of the measure. If a point of order is sustained, the offending provision is stricken from the conference report. After all points of order have been dealt with, the Senate decides whether to send to the House the remaining text of the conference report. The decision is debatable under the same limitations that may apply to the conference report, and no amendments are allowed. The Senate may waive this point of order with regard to a single provision or all provisions constituting new directed spending or appeal the Presiding Officer's ruling by a supermajority vote. Three-fifths of all Senators must vote to waive the rule or overrule the Presiding Officer's decision.

Under this Senate rule, any Senator may propose a motion to waive all points of order provided in this rule with respect to a pending measure or motion. A three-fifths vote of all Senators is required to adopt the motion. All motions to waive all such points of order against the pending measure or motion are collectively debatable for no more than one hour, equally divided and controlled by the Senate Majority and Minority Leaders (or their designees). Such motions are not amendable.

EARMARKS AND LEVERAGE

The House rule prohibits a Member from conditioning the inclusion of an earmark in a measure, conference report, or report language on any vote cast by another Member.[36] There is no similar Senate requirement.

End Notes

[1] This report uses the term *earmark* to apply to a "congressional earmark" as used in the House rule and "congressionally directed spending item" as used in the Senate rule, as well as "limited tax or tariff benefits" (see below, "Earmark Definition" section).

[2] Section 404 of H.Res. 6 (110th Congress) added new clause 9 to House Rule XXI and two new clause (16 and 17) to House rule XXIII.

[3] Section 2(i) of H.Res. 5 (111th Congress).

[4] 121 Stat. 735, 760. Section 521 established Senate Rule XLIV. Additionally, section 511 amended Senate Rule XXVIII, *Conference Committees; Reports; Open Meetings*, to significantly alter the procedure for disposing of points of order against "out of scope material" in conference reports (121 Stat. 735, 757). For more information, see CRS Report RS22733, *Senate Rules Restricting the Content of Conference Reports*, by Elizabeth Rybicki.

[5] The Senate Appropriations Committee, for example, has stated that it will require Members requesting earmarks to post information regarding their earmark requests on their personal website. This information must be posted at the time of the request and must include the purpose of the earmark and why it is a valuable use of taxpayer funds. (As stated in the January 6, 2009 joint press release from the House and Senate Appropriations Committees Chairmen titled, *House and Senate Appropriations Committees Announce Additional Reforms in Committee Earmark Policy*, available at http://appropriations

Committees may also establish relevant administrative or policy requirements (e.g., prioritizing requests, submitting requests in electronic form, or requiring matching funds for earmark requests) or restrictions (e.g., not considering earmark requests for certain appropriations accounts or disallowing multi-year funding requests). In addition, committees and subcommittees often have deadlines, especially for earmark requests in appropriations legislation. Such requirements may be communicated through a "Dear Colleague" letter, committee staff memo, or through the committee's website. For this reason, it is important to check with individual committees and subcommittees to learn of any supplemental earmark request requirements or restrictions. For a discussion of considerations for Members submitting earmark requests, see CRS Report RS22866, *Earmark Disclosure Rules in the House: Member and Committee Requirements*, by Megan Suzanne Lynch and CRS Report RS22867, *Earmark Disclosure Rules in the Senate: Member and Committee Requirements*, by Megan Suzanne Lynch.

[6] Under Executive Order 13457, issued in January 2008, executive agencies were directed not to commit obligate, or expend funds that were the result of an earmark included in non-statutory language, such as a committee report. For further information, see "Protecting American Taxpayers From Governmental Spending on Wasteful Earmarks," Executive Order 13,457, January 29, 2008, available at http://www.whitehouse.gov/news/releases/2008/01/20080129- 5.html and CRS Report RL34373, *Earmarks Executive Order: Legal Issues*, by Thomas J. Nicola and T. J. Halstead.

[7] House Rule XXI, clause 9(d) and Senate Rule XLIV, paragraph 5.

[8] The term *report language* refers to information provided in reports accompanying committee-reported legislation as well as joint explanatory statements, which are attached to conference reports. Although the entire document is generally referred to as a conference report, it comprises two separate parts. The conference report contains a conference committee's proposal for legislative language resolving the House and Senate differences on a measure, while the joint explanatory statement explains the conference report. If enacted, the bill text has statutory effect; the joint explanatory statement does not.

[9] Examples of an entity include a specific university or college, unit of a local or state government, or museum.

[10] For more on miscellaneous bills, see CRS Report RL33 867, *Tariff Modifications: Miscellaneous Tariff Bills*, by Vivian C. Jones.

[11] This provision applies to any Representative, Delegate, or the Resident Commissioner requesting an earmark on the list. The name of any Senator requesting such an earmark that appears in a conference report or accompanying joint explanatory statement is also required.

[12] A *committee of initial referral* refers to each committee to which a legislative measure is referred upon introduction of the legislation. In the House, bills are sometimes initially referred to more than one committee. The rule does not, however, cover committee(s) to which a bill is referred after an initial referral(s).

[13] Letter from the Office of the Parliamentarian to the Committee on Rules, inserted in the *Congressional Record* by Rep. Sessions, *Congressional Record*, daily edition, vol. 153, October 3, 2007, pp. H1 1184-H1 1185.

[14] To resolve differences between the House- and Senate-passed versions of a measure, Congress may refer the measure to a conference committee or, in other circumstances, Congress may consider amendments between the Houses.

[15] In this situation, a special rule provides for a committee amendment to replace the entire text of the measure and allows that committee amendment to be subsequently amended in two degrees, as if it were the original text of the measure. For more information, see CRS Report 98-995, *The Amending Process in the House of Representatives*, by Christopher M. Davis.

[16] For more details, see CRS Report RS22015, *Availability of Legislative Measures in the House of Representatives (The "Three-Day Rule")*, by Elizabeth Rybicki.

[17] Ibid.

[18] House Rule XXI, clause 9(c).

[19] *Congressional Record*, daily edition, vol. 153, May 10, 2007, p. H4880.

[20] The method of resolving a point of order by a question of consideration is similar to that provided in Section 426 of the Congressional Budget Act for dealing with special rules that waive the application of Section 425 of the act prohibiting the consideration of legislation that includes an unfunded federal intergovernmental mandate.

[21] Points of order raised under this requirement are based solely on whether the rule includes a waiver of Rule XXI, clause 9, and not whether such a waiver is necessary. For example, a point of order was raised against the consideration of a special rule providing for consideration of the conference report for the Department of Defense appropriations act for FY2008 because it waived all rules of the House, including Rule XXI, clause 9 and H.Res. 491. *Congressional Record*, daily edition, vol. 153, November 8, 2007, pp. H13312-H13314.

[22] The Senate typically decides to consider a measure by unanimous consent, but may also do so by a motion to proceed, which requires a majority vote to adopt. House-passed measures not reported from a Senate committee are not included because they do not include earmarks requested by Senators.

[23] Under the rule, the certification authority rests with the Majority Leader (or his designee) and committee chairs, not subcommittee chairs.

[24] For general information on points of order in the Senate, see CRS Report 98-306, *Points of Order, Rulings, and Appeals in the Senate*, by Valerie Heitshusen.

[25] Ibid.

[26] Senate Rule XLIV, paragraph 12.

[27] An additional earmark is one that is not included in the measure as placed on the Senate calendar or as reported by a committee or included in any accompanying committee report.

[28] House Rule XXIII, clause 17, and Senate Rule XLIV, paragraph 6.

[29] The Senate rule requires the "name and location" of the intended recipient.

[30] For more information on the Senate pecuniary interest certification requirement, see Senate Select Committee on Ethics, Dear Colleague Letter, *Definition of "Immediate Family" for Requested Appropriations*, September 12, 2007, available at http://ethics.senate.gov/. For more information on the House requirement, guidance and clarification in determining a financial interest is available in U.S. Congress, House Committee on Standards of Official Conduct, *The House Ethics Manual*, 110th Cong., 2nd sess., 2008, (Washington: GPO, 2008), pp. 238-239. Available also at http://ethics.house.gov/Media/PDF/2008_House_Ethics_Manual.pdf.

[31] Congress considers 12 annual regular appropriations bills.

[32] This paragraph applies to any Representative, Delegate, Resident Commissioner, as well as any Senator.

[33] Clause 9 also prohibits consideration of a special rule waiving this requirement.

[34] For more information, see CRS Report RS22733, *Senate Rules Restricting the Content of Conference Reports*, by Elizabeth Rybicki.

[35] Each account, generally, includes similar programs, projects, or items, such as a "research and development" account or "salaries and expenses" account. For small agencies, a single account may fund all of the agency's activities. These acts typically provide a lump-sum amount for each of these accounts. A few accounts include a single program, project, or item, which the appropriations acts fund individually.

[36] House Standing Rule XXIII, clause 16. While there is no point of order established under this provision, an alleged violation may give rise to a collateral challenge in the form of a question of the privileges of the House pursuant to Rule IX. See, for example, consideration of H.Res. 1040 (110th Congress) in the *Congressional Record*, daily edition, vol. 154, March 12, 2008, pp. H1552-H1553.

In: Earmarks: Disclosure, Legal Developments… ISBN: 978-1-61324-588-0
Editors: Roger D. Halstead

Chapter 4

EARMARKS EXECUTIVE ORDER: LEGAL ISSUES

Thomas J. Nicola and T.J. Halstead

SUMMARY

On January 29, 2008, President George W. Bush signed Executive Order 13,457, "Protecting American Taxpayers from Government Spending on Wasteful Earmarks." The order states that it is the policy of the federal government "to be judicious in the expenditure of taxpayer dollars." In order "[t]o ensure the proper use of taxpayer funds," the order provides that the number and cost of earmarks should be reduced, that their origin and purposes should be transparent; and that they should be included in the text of bills voted upon by Congress and presented to the President. For appropriations laws and other legislation enacted after the date of the order, it directs executive agencies not to commit, obligate, or expend funds on the basis of earmarks included in any non-statutory source, including requests in reports of committees of Congress or other congressional documents or communications on behalf of Members of Congress, or any other non-statutory source, except when required by law or when an agency itself has determined that a project, program, grant, or other transaction has merit under statutory criteria or other merit-based decision-making.

In the context of the order, an "earmark" is defined as any

> funds provided by Congress for projects, programs, or grants where the purported congressional direction (whether in statutory text, report language, or other communication) circumvents otherwise applicable merit-based or competitive allocation processes, or specifies the location or recipient, or otherwise curtails the ability of the executive branch to manage its statutory and constitutional responsibilities pertaining to the funds allocation process.

There is a long tradition of congressional inclusion of, and agency compliance with, spending directives that are delineated in committee report language or in joint explanatory statements issued by conference committees. If applied rigorously, the provisions of Executive Order 13,457 could significantly alter this traditional dynamic. Accordingly, this report provides an overview of the provisions of the order; addresses questions that have arisen regarding both the President's authority to control executive branch activity in this context and the effect of non-statutory congressional spending directives; and considers and evaluates potential congressional responses to the executive order.

INTRODUCTION

On January 29, 2008, President George W. Bush signed Executive Order 13,457, "Protecting American Taxpayers from Government Spending on Wasteful Earmarks."[1] The order states that it is the policy of the federal government "to be judicious in the expenditure of taxpayer dollars." In order "[t]o ensure the proper use of taxpayer funds," the order provides that the number and cost of earmarks should be reduced, that their origin and purposes should be transparent, and that they should be included in the text of bills voted upon by Congress and presented to the President.[2] For appropriations laws and other legislation enacted after the date of the order, it directs executive agencies not to commit, obligate, or expend funds on the basis of earmarks included in any non-statutory source, including requests in reports of committees of Congress or other congressional documents or communications on behalf of Members of Congress, or any other non-statutory source, except when required by law or when an agency itself has determined that a project, program, grant, or other transaction has merit under statutory criteria or other merit-based decision-making.[3]

Under the executive order, an "agency" is an executive agency defined in section 105 of title 5 of the United States Code and includes the United States Postal Service and the Postal Regulatory Commission, but excludes the Government Accountability Office.[4] This section states that an "executive agency" means a "department, a government corporation, and an independent establishment." An "independent establishment" is defined in section 104 of title 5.[5]

An "earmark" in the executive order means

> funds provided by Congress for projects, programs, or grants where the purported congressional direction (whether in statutory text, report language, or other communication) circumvents otherwise applicable merit-based or competitive allocation processes, or specifies the location or recipient, or otherwise curtails the ability of the executive branch to manage its statutory and constitutional responsibilities pertaining to the funds allocation process.[6]

The executive order identifies four duties of agency heads relating to earmarks. With respect to all appropriations laws and other legislation enacted after the date of the order, it directs the each agency head to take all necessary steps to ensure, first, that

> (1) agency decisions to commit, obligate, or expend funds for any earmark are based on the text of laws, and are not based on language in any congressional committee report, joint explanatory statement of a committee of conference, statement of managers concerning a bill in Congress, or any other non-statutory statement or indication of views of Congress or a House of Congress, committee, Member, officer, or staff thereof;
> (2) agency decisions to commit, obligate, or expend funds for any earmark are based on authorized, transparent, statutory criteria and merit-based decisionmaking, in the manner set forth in section II of Office of Management and Budget (OMB) Memorandum M-07-10, dated February 15, 2007,[7] to the extent consistent with applicable law; and
> (3) no oral or written communications concerning earmarks shall supersede statutory criteria, competitive awards, or merit-based decisionmaking.[8]

Second, the executive order provides that an agency shall not consider the views of a House of Congress, committee, Member, officer, or staff of

Congress with respect to commitments, obligations, or expenditures to carry out any earmark unless such views are in writing, to facilitate consideration in accordance with the requirement to base spending decisions on authorized, transparent statutory criteria and merit-based decision making to the extent consistent with applicable law. All written communications from Congress, a House of Congress, committee, Member, officer, or staff thereof, recommending that funds be committed, obligated, or expended on any earmark shall be made publicly available on the Internet by the receiving agency, not later than 30 days after such communication is received, unless otherwise specifically directed by the agency head, without delegation, after consulting with the OMB Director, to preserve appropriate confidentiality between the executive and legislative branches.[9]

Third, it requires that agency heads otherwise shall implement within their respective agencies the policy set forth in § 1 of the executive order consistent with any instructions that the Director of OMB may prescribe.[10]

The fourth duty is to provide to the OMB Director any information about earmarks and compliance with the executive order that the Director requests.[11]

Executive Order 13,457 has some general provisions which state that nothing in it shall be construed to impair or otherwise affect: (a) authority granted by law to an agency or agency head;[12] or (b) functions of the OMB Director relating to budget, administrative, or legislative proposals.[13] Moreover, it provides that the order shall be implemented in a manner consistent with applicable law and subject to the availability of appropriations.[14] Finally, the order is not intended to, and does not, create any right or benefit, substantive or procedural, enforceable at law or in equity, by any party against the United States, its agencies, instrumentalities, its officers, employees, or agents, or any other person.[15]

In his State of the Union address on January 28, 2008, the President explained the reason for issuing the executive order:

> The people's trust in their government is undermined by congressional earmarks — special interest projects that are often stuck in at the last minute, without discussion or debate. Last year I asked you to voluntarily cut the number of earmarks and the cost of earmarks in half. I also asked you to stop slipping earmarks into committee reports that never come to a vote. Unfortunately, neither goal was met. So this time, if you send me an appropriations bill that does not cut the number or cost of earmarks in half, I'll send it back to you with my veto. And tomorrow, I will issue an executive order that directs federal agencies to ignore any future earmark that is not voted

on by Congress. If these items are truly worth funding, Congress should debate them in the open and hold a public vote.[16]

PRESIDENTIAL AUTHORITY TO ISSUE EXECUTIVE ORDERS AND THEIR LEGAL EFFECT

There is a long tradition of congressional inclusion of, and agency compliance with, spending directives that are delineated in committee report language or in joint explanatory statements issued by conference committees. If applied rigorously, the provisions of Executive Order 13,457 could significantly alter this traditional dynamic, raising questions regarding the President's authority to control executive branch activity in this context via executive order.

The President's ability to issue and implement executive orders may stem from both constitutional and statutory authority. In the constitutional context, presidential power to issue such orders has been derived from Article II, which states that "the executive power shall be vested in a President of the United States," that "the President shall be Commander in Chief of the Army and Navy of the United States," and that the President "shall take care that the laws be faithfully executed."[17] The President's power to issue executive orders and proclamations may also derive from express or implied statutory authority.[18] Irrespective of the nature of the authority to issue executive orders and proclamations, these instruments have been employed by every President since the inception of the Republic, and Presidents have not hesitated to wield this power over a wide range of often controversial subjects.[19] Furthermore, if issued under a valid claim of authority and published, these instruments may have the force and effect of law, requiring courts to take judicial notice of their existence.[20]

While these principles establish the authority of the President to issue executive orders generally, the question of whether a particular order comports with constitutional and statutory provisions requires a more nuanced analysis. The framework for analyzing the validity of an executive order was delineated in *Youngstown Sheet & Tube Co. v. Sawyer*.[21] There, the Supreme Court dealt with President Truman's executive order directing the seizure of steel mills, which was issued in an effort to avert the effects of a workers' strike during the Korean War. Invalidating this action, the majority held that under the Constitution, "the President's power to see that laws are faithfully executed refutes the idea that he is to be a lawmaker."[22] Specifically, Justice Black maintained that Presidential authority to issue such an executive order "must stem either from an act of Congress or from the Constitution itself."[23] Applying this reasoning, Justice Black's opinion for the Court determined that as no statute or Constitutional provision authorized such presidential action, the seizure order was in essence a legislative act. The Court further noted that Congress had rejected seizure as a means to settle labor disputes during consideration of the Taft-Hartley Act. Given this characterization, the Court deemed the executive order to be an unconstitutional violation of the separation of powers doctrine, explaining "the founders of this Nation entrusted the lawmaking power to the Congress alone in both good and bad times."[24]

While Justice Black's majority opinion in *Youngstown* seems to refute the notion that the President possesses implied constitutional powers, there were five concurrences in the case, four of which maintained that implied presidential authority adheres in certain contexts.[25] Of these concurrences, Justice Jackson's has proven to be the most influential, even surpassing the impact of Justice Black's majority opinion. Specifically, Justice Jackson established a tri-partite scheme for analyzing the validity of presidential actions in relation to constitutional and congressional authority.[26]

Justice Jackson's first category focuses on whether the President has acted according to an express or implied grant of congressional authority. If so, according to Jackson, presidential "authority is at its maximum, for it includes all that he possesses in his own right plus all that Congress can delegate," and such action is "supported by the strongest of presumptions and the widest latitude of judicial interpretation."[27] Secondly, Justice Jackson maintained that, in situations where Congress has neither granted nor denied authority to the President, the President acts in reliance only "upon his own independent powers, but there is a zone of twilight in which he and Congress may have concurrent authority, or in which its distribution is uncertain."[28] In the third and final category, Justice Jackson stated that in instances where presidential action is "incompatible with the express or implied will of Congress," the power of the President is at its minimum, and any such action may be supported pursuant only the President's "own constitutional powers minus any constitutional powers of Congress over the matter."[29] In such a circumstance, presidential action must rest upon an exclusive power, and the Courts can uphold the measure "only by disabling the Congress from acting upon the subject."[30]

With regard to President Truman's order, Justice Jackson determined that analysis under the first category was inappropriate, due to the fact that seizure of steel mills had not been authorized by Congress, either implicitly or explicitly. Justice Jackson also determined that the second category was "clearly eliminated," in that Congress had addressed the issue of seizure, through statutory policies conflicting with the President's actions.[31] Employing the third category, Justice Jackson noted that President Truman's actions could only be sustained by determining that the seizure was "within his domain and beyond control by Congress."[32] Justice Jackson concluded that such matters were not outside the scope of congressional power, reinforcing his declaration that permitting the President to exercise such "conclusive and preclusive" power would endanger "the equilibrium established by our constitutional system."[33]

Applying these principles to the case at hand, there does not appear to be any discernible basis upon which it could be asserted that Executive Order 13,457 runs contrary to constitutional or statutory precepts. While the potential centralization of control over agency treatment of non-statutory earmarks raises significant policy issues, E.O. 13,457 appears to fall within the accepted parameters of presidential authority in the executive order context, particularly when viewed in relation to other executive orders that have asserted similar and arguably more expansive centralization authority.

For instance, in 1981, President Reagan issued Executive Order 12,291, ushering in a new era of presidential control over agency rulemaking activity.[34] E.O. 12,291 required cost-benefit analyses and established a centralized review procedure for all agency regulations. E.O. 12,291 delegated responsibility for this clearance requirement to the Office of Information and Regulatory Affairs, which had recently been created within the Office of Management and Budget as part of the Paperwork Reduction Act of 1980. The impact of E.O. 12,291 on agency regulatory activities was immediate and substantial, generating controversy and criticism. Opponents of the order asserted that review thereunder was distinctly anti-regulatory and constituted an unconstitutional transfer of authority from the executive agencies.[35] Despite these concerns, courts considering OMB involvement in agency rulemaking under the executive order did not address the constitutionality of such review,[36] and Congress did not act to countermand the executive order. The review scheme established in the Reagan Administration has been employed and modified by subsequent Administrations in a manner that conveys a conception of presidential authority consonant with that of the Reagan order.[37] However, arguments against the constitutionality of these executive orders have largely diminished, to the point that presidential review of agency rulemaking has become a widely used and increasingly accepted mechanism by which a President can exert significant and sometimes determinative authority over the agency rulemaking process.[38]

The implicit acquiescence of Congress and the courts regarding the constitutionality of 12,291 and its successors indicates that a President may successfully utilize executive orders to exert significant, centralized control over executive branch activity that has traditionally been exercised at the departmental or agency level. This rationale seems fully applicable to Executive Order 13,457, particularly in light of the fact that non-statutory earmarks are not legally binding on executive branch agencies.

Consistency between Executive Order and Existing Case Law Regarding Report Language

Art. I, sec. 9, cl. 7 of the Constitution states that, "No money shall be drawn from the treasury, but in consequence of appropriations made by law." With respect to all appropriations laws and other legislation enacted after the date of the order, the executive order directs each agency head to take all necessary steps to ensure that agency spending decisions are based on the text of laws and not on language in legislative history documents or other congressional communications to agencies and otherwise to implement the policy that earmarks should be included in the text of bills voted upon by Congress and presented to the President.

The Supreme Court in *Lincoln* v. *Vigil*[39] unanimously acknowledged a premise upon which the executive order appears to be based: Language in legislative history documents does not legally bind agencies unless it is enacted in the text of a statute.

> [A] fundamental principle of appropriations law is that where "Congress merely appropriates lump sum amounts without statutorily restricting what can be done with those funds, a clear inference arises that it does not intend to impose legally binding restrictions, and indicia in committee reports and other legislative history as to how funds should or are expected to be spent do not establish any legal requirements on" the agency. *LTV Aerospace Corp.*, 55 Comp. Gen. 307, 309 (1975); *cf.*, *American Hospital Assn. v. NLRB*, 499 U.S. 606, 616 (1991) (statements in committee reports do not have the force of law); *TVA v. Hill,* 437 U.S. 153, 191 (1978) ("Expressions of committees dealing with requests for appropriations cannot be

> equated with statutes enacted by Congress.") Put another way, a lump sum appropriation reflects a congressional recognition that an agency must be allowed "flexibility to shift ... funds within a particular ... appropriation account so that" the agency "can make necessary adjustments for 'unforeseen developments' and 'changing requirements.'" *LTV Aerospace Corp., supra*, at 318 (citation omitted.)" ... Of course, an agency is not free simply to disregard statutory responsibilities: Congress may always circumscribe agency discretion to allocate resources by putting restrictions in the operative statutes (though not, as we have seen, just in the legislative history).[40]

A year later in *Shannon* v, *United States*,[41] the Court emphasized this point when it observed that, "We are not aware of any case ... in which we have given authoritative weight to a single passage of legislative history that is in no way anchored in the text of a statute.... We agree with the D.C. Circuit that "Courts have no authority to enforce [a] principl[e] gleaned solely from legislative history that has no statutory reference point."[42]

The Court in the *Lincoln* case quoted from *LTV Aerospace Corp.*, a decision of the Comptroller General, who heads the Government Accountability Office (GAO), formerly the General Accounting Office. In that decision, the Comptroller General said that

> with respect to appropriations, there is a clear distinction to be made between the imposition of statutory restrictions or conditions which are intended to be legally binding and the technique of specifying restrictions or conditions in a nonstatutory context.
>
> In this regard, Congress has recognized that in most instances it is desirable to maintain executive flexibility to shift around funds within a particular lump sum so that agencies can make necessary adjustments.... This is not to say that Congress does not expect that funds will be spent in accordance with budget estimates or in accordance with restrictions detailed in committee reports. However, in order to preserve spending flexibility, it may choose not to impose those particular restrictions as a matter of law, but rather to leave it to the agencies to "keep faith" with the Congress.... There are practical reasons why agencies can be expected to comply with these congressional expectations....
>
> On the other hand, when Congress does not intend to permit agency flexibility, but intends to impose a legally binding restriction on an agency's use of funds, it does so by means of explicit statutory language.[43]

The Comptroller General added that

> as a general proposition, there is a distinction to be made between utilizing legislative history for the purpose of illuminating underlying language and resorting to that history for the purpose of writing into law that which is not there....
>
> An accommodation has developed between the Congress and the executive branch resulting in the appropriation process flexibility discussed above. Funds are most often appropriated in lump sums on the basis of mutual legislative and executive understandings as to their use and derive from agency budget estimates and testimony and expressions of intent in committee reports. The understandings reached generally are not engrafted upon the appropriation provisions enacted. *To establish as a matter of law specific restrictions covering the detailed and complete basis upon which appropriated funds are understood to be provided would, as a practical matter, severely limit the capability of agencies to accommodate changing conditions.*[44]

Both the Supreme Court and the Comptroller General have indicated the consequence for an agency if it disregards directives in legislative history documents. The Court in the *Lincoln* case said that, "And, of course, we hardly need to note that an agency's decision to ignore congressional expectations may expose it to grave political consequences."[45] Referring to a passage which indicated that Congress sometimes places restrictions in legislative history documents rather than in statutory text to permit agencies to accommodate changing conditions when allocating funds, the Comptroller General stated that, "This does not mean agencies are free to ignore clearly expressed legislative history applicable to the use of appropriated funds. They ignore such expressions of intent at the peril of strained relations with the Congress. The executive branch ... has a practical duty to abide by such expressions. This duty, however, must be understood to fall short of a statutory requirement giving rise to a legal infraction where there is a failure to carry out that duty."[46]

CONGRESSIONAL RESPONSE TO EXECUTIVE ORDER

The above sections have reviewed the elements of Executive Order 13,457, the legal basis for the President to issue executive orders and their legal effect, and the consistency between the substance of the order and case law which acknowledges that earmarks in legislative history documents but not in statutory text do not legally bind agencies to fund them. A primary purpose of the executive order appears to be to limit the discretion of individual executive agency heads to fund earmarks that appear only in legislative history documents and other nonstatutory sources; it expresses a uniform policy throughout the executive branch that they generally should not be funded and that agency heads should base funding decisions on "authorized, transparent, statutory criteria and merit-based decision-making."

Congress has a number of options to respond to this executive order. It can choose to operate within the new legal milieu that it appears to formalize or take steps to countermand it. One option to operate within it, of course, would be for Congress expressly to include each earmark in the text of a statute and thereby place it beyond the agency decision-making process that the executive order requires for nonstatutory ones. To become law, each earmark in a bill would have to pass the House and Senate and be presented to the President and, if the bill were vetoed, pass by two-thirds of each House to override a presidential veto. Another form of express incorporation would be for Congress to include language in a statute to the effect that, "Earmarks in a joint explanatory statement in House Report No. 1 10-XXX shall be effective as if enacted into law."

Another option would be for Congress to incorporate by reference in the text of a statute each earmark that appears in legislative history documents in such a way that Members and Senators voting on the incorporating textual language and the President to whom the language is presented would be made aware of the earmarks involved. An example is a provision of the Revised Continuing Appropriations Resolution, 2007,[47] which provides that, "The Office of National Drug Control Policy shall expend funds for 'Counterdrug Technology Center' by Public Law 109-115 in accordance with the joint explanatory statement of the committee of conference (H.Rept. No. 109-307) within 60 days after the date of enactment of this section."[48]

The unambiguous language of a directive of this type — "shall expend" — would appear legally to bind an agency to expend funds in accordance with the joint explanatory statement to which the directive refers. In *Chevron, U.S.A.* v. *Natural Resources Defense Council, Inc.*,[49] the Supreme Court held that

> [w]hen a court reviews an agency's construction of a statute, it is confronted with two questions. First, always, is the question whether Congress has directly spoken to the precise question at issue. If the intent of Congress is clear, that is the end of the matter, for the court,

as well as the agency, must give effect to the unambiguously expressed intent of Congress.[50]

A passage in the policy section of the earmarks executive order may acknowledge this principle. It states, in relevant part, that "[f]or appropriations laws and other legislation enacted after the date of this order, executive agencies should not commit, obligate, or expend funds on the basis of earmarks included in any non- statutory source, including reports of committees of the Congress or other congressional documents ... except when required by law."

If Congress should choose to attempt to countermand the executive order, it could seek to enact language stating that it should have no force and effect. Another congressional option would be to seek to deny funds to the Office of Management and Budget to enforce the order. As noted above, § 4(b) of the order states that it "... shall be implemented in a manner consistent with applicable law and subject to the availability of appropriations." There is precedent for Congress enacting a statute to revoke an executive order. During the Administration of President William J. Clinton, Congress enacted a provision of the National Institutes of Health Revitalization Act of 1993, which stated that the provisions of Executive Order 12,806,[51] "... shall not have any legal effect."[52] This executive order, which had been issued by President George H.W. Bush the previous year, directed the Secretary of Health and Human Services to establish a fetal tissue bank. Given the highly speculative basis of any asserted constitutional authority for the President to issue such an order, there appears to be little doubt as to the legitimacy of this congressional revocation.[53] However, any congressional attempt to revoke the earmarks executive order could set the stage for a more significant confrontation, given the broad conception of presidential authority upon which its issuance appears to be premised.[54]

Ultimately, whether enacting a statute to revoke the order or enacting language denying OMB funds to enforce it would have significant legal effect is not clear because of the nature of the order. As noted in the discussion above on consistency between it and relevant case law, Executive Order 13,457 does not appear to create new law. Instead, it directs executive agencies to comply with a principle acknowledged by the Supreme Court: namely, that agencies are not legally required to fund earmarks contained in legislative documents but not in the text of statutes. Its significance appears to be in the establishment of a uniform policy throughout the executive branch and the imposition of specific duties on agency heads to foster its implementation.

CONCLUSION

The provisions of Executive Order 13,457 may significantly influence the dynamic that has traditionally governed executive and legislative practice with regard to nonstatutory earmarks, but the order itself appears to fall within the accepted parameters of presidential authority in the executive order context. Courts have acknowledged a premise upon which the order appears to be based: Earmarks in legislative history documents and other sources that are not anchored in statutory text have no legal force or effect. Moreover, while the provisions of the order appear to direct executive agencies to refrain from funding nonstatutory earmarks that they may have funded as a matter of course before it was issued, Congress has options such as expressly including earmarks in the texts of statutes or statutorily incorporating by reference earmarks in legislative history documents. These congressional responses may ameliorate the impact of the order. Ultimately, the extent to which the earmarks executive order will affect agency practice pertaining to non-statutory earmarks remains to be seen, and, as the foregoing analysis indicates, may prove to be more a matter of political rather than legal significance.

End Notes

1 Exec. Order 13,457, 73 Fed. Reg. 6417 (February 1, 2008).
2 *Id.* at § 1.
3 *Id.* at § 1.
4 *Id.* at § 3.
5 This provision defines an "independent establishment" as "an establishment in the executive branch (other than the United States Postal Service or the Postal Regulatory Commission) which is not an Executive department, military department, Government corporation, or part thereof, or part of an independent establishment," and "the Government Accountability Office." 5 U.S.C. § 104(1)-(2).
6 *Id.* at § 4.
7 OMB Memorandum M-07-10 is available at Memoranda at [http://www.whitehouse. gov/omb] by number and date, February 15, 2007.
8 Exec. Order 13,457, § 2(a).
9 *Id.* at § 2(b).
10 *Id.* at § 2(c).
11 *Id.* at § 2(d).
12 *Id.* at § 4(a)(I).
13 *Id.* at § 4(a)(ii).
14 *Id.* at § 4(b).
15 *Id.* at § 4(c).
16 The State of the Union transcript is available at [http://www.whitehouse.gov], *see* Newsm, by date, January 28, 2008.
17 U.S. Const., Art. II, §1, 2, & 3.

[18] *See* Youngstown Sheet and Tube Co. v. Sawyer, 343 U.S. 579 (1952).

[19] *See* CRS Report RS20846, *Executive Orders: Issuance and Revocation*, by T. J. Halstead (2001).

[20] Armstrong v. United States, 80 U.S. 154 (1871); *see also,* Farkas v. Texas Instrument, Inc., 372 F.2d 629 (5th Cir. 1967); Farmer v. Philadelphia Electric Co., 329 F.2d 3 (3rd Cir. 1964); Jenkins v. Collard, 145 U.S. 546, 560-6 1 (1893).

[21] 343 U.S. 579 (1952).

[22] *Id.* at 587.

[23] *Id.* at 585.

[24] *Id.* at 586-589.

[25] *Id.* at 659 (Burton, J., concurring); *Id.* at 661 (Clark, J., concurring in result only); *Id.* at 610 (Frankfurter, J., concurring); *Id.* at 635 (Jackson, J., concurring).

[26] *Id.* at 635-638.

[27] *Id.* at 635, 637.

[28] *Id.* at 637.

[29] *Id.* at 637.

[30] *Id.* at 637-638.

[31] *Id.* at 638-639.

[32] *Id.* at 640.

[33] *Id.* at 638, 640-645.

[34] Exec. Order 12,291, 46 Fed. Reg. 13,193 (February 17, 1981).

[35] For a thorough overview of the criticisms leveled at the Reagan order, *see* Richard H. Pildes, Cass R. Sunstein, "Reinventing the Regulatory State," 62 U. Chi. L. Rev. 1, 4-6 (1995); Elena Kagan, "Presidential Administration," n.10, *supra*, at 2279-80. *But see*, Frank B. Cross, "Executive Orders 12,2291 and 12,498: A Test Case in Presidential Control of Executive Agencies," 4 J.L & Pol. 483 (1988) (supporting constitutionality and utility of review under the order).

[36] In Public Citizen Health Research Group v. Tyson, 796 F.2d 1479 (D.C. Cir. 1986), for instance, the court addressed the validity of a rule promulgated by OSHA governing ethylene oixide, including a challenge based on the argument that a critical portion of the proposed rule had been deleted based on a command from OMB. While stating that "OMB's participation in the rulemaking presents difficult constitutional questions concerning the executive's proper role in administrative proceedings and the appropriate scope of delegated power from Congress to certain executive agencies," the court nonetheless found that it had "no occasion to reach the difficult constitutional questions presented by OMB's participation." *Id.* at 1507.

[37] *See* CRS Report RL32855, *Presidential Review of Agency Rulemaking*, by T. J. Halstead(2005).

[38] *Id.*

[39] 508 U.S. 182 (1993).

[40] 508 U.S. at 192-193.

[41] 512 U.S. 573 (1994).

[42] 512 U.S. at 583, *quoting from* International Brotherhood of Electrical Workers v. National Labor Relations Board, 814 F.2d 697, 712 (D.C.Cir.1987)

[43] LTV Aerospace Corp., 55 Comp. Gen. 307, 325 (1975) (footnote omitted).

[44] *Id.* at 325-326 (Emphasis supplied.).

[45] 508 U.S. at 193.

[46] 55 Comp. Gen. at 326.

[47] P.L. 110-5, 121 Stat. 8 (2007).

[48] *Id.,* chap. 10, § 21057(b), 121 Stat. at 55.

[49] 467 U.S. 837 (1984); *reh. denied*, 468 U.S. 1227 (1984).

[50] 467 U.S. at 842-843.

[51] Exec. Order 12,806, 57 Fed. Reg. 21,589 (May 21, 1992).

[52] P.L. 103-43, §121, 107 Stat. 133 (June 10, 1993).
[53] *See Youngstown*, 343 U.S. at 635-638.
[54] *See* n. 37, *supra*, at 3.

In: Earmarks: Disclosure, Legal Developments… ISBN: 978-1-61324-588-0
Editors: Roger D. Halstead

Chapter 5

EARMARKS DISCLOSED BY CONGRESS: FY2008-FY2010 REGULAR APPROPRIATIONS BILLS

Carol Hardy Vincent and Jim Monke

SUMMARY

In 2007, both the House and the Senate established new earmark transparency procedures. They provide for public disclosure of approved earmarks and the identification of their congressional sponsors. These procedures currently are contained in House Rule XXI, clause 9, and Senate Rule XLIV. Under both chambers' rules, an earmark is a provision in legislation or report language that is included primarily at the request of a Member, and provides, authorizes, or recommends a specific amount to an entity or to a specific state, locality, or congressional district.

This report summarizes the earmarks disclosed for the 12 regular, annual appropriations bills for each of FY2008, FY2009, and FY2010. For these bills, a list of earmarks was typically included in the explanatory statement accompanying the final version of the bill under the heading "Disclosure of Earmarks and Congressionally Directed Spending Items." This report does not pertain to any earmarks disclosed in supplemental appropriations or authorizing legislation.

This report directly analyzes the data in the earmark disclosure lists, without additions or deletions. For individual earmarks, the disclosures typically identify the federal agency, project name, amount, and requester. In some cases, other information also has been included, such as an account within an agency, or the purpose or location of the earmark.

In FY2010, Congress identified 11,320 earmarks with a total value of \$32.0 billion. Some appropriations bills account for more earmarks than others (**Table 2**). For instance, about four- fifths of the 11,320 earmarks in FY2010 are in five of the 12 appropriations bills. The Energy and Water Development and Related Agencies appropriations bill contains the greatest number of FY2010 earmarks—2,293, about 20% of the total number of earmarks.

The distribution of the value of earmarks is more concentrated, with about \$27.5 billion, or 86%, of the value of earmarks in four of the appropriations bills. The Military Construction and Veterans Affairs and Related Agencies appropriations bill contains the greatest value of FY2010 earmarks—\$14.5 billion, about 45% of the total value. Some appropriations bills account for fewer earmarks but have a greater share of the value, or vice versa.

House and Senate rules do not require congressional disclosure of presidentially requested earmarks. However, nine appropriations bills in FY20 10 list the President as a requester, either solely or with a Member of Congress, for 2,039 earmarks worth \$21.8 billion (18% of the total number and 68% of the total value of earmarks in the disclosure lists). It is possible that there are more presidential earmarks than those disclosed by Congress. There were 9,281 Member-only earmarks worth \$10.2 billion (82% of the total number and 32% of the total value, **Table 3**).

From FY2008 to FY2010, the total number of appropriations earmarks in all 12 bills decreased 12%, from 12,810 to 11,320. However, the total value of earmarks increased 11%, from \$28.9 billion to \$32.0 billion (**Table 5**). The percentage of the total appropriation that was earmarked decreased from 1.8% in FY2008 to 1.5% in FY2010. Excluding mandatory spending, the percentage of non-mandatory appropriations that were earmarked fell from 2.9% to 2.4%. Both the number and value of President-only earmarks increased since FY2008 (from 819 earmarks worth \$4.2 billion in FY2008, to 1,265 earmarks worth \$9.5 billion in FY2010; up 54% by number and 126% by value). Conversely, the number and value of Member-only earmarks decreased since FY2008, from 11,117 earmarks worth \$12.5 billion in FY2008, to 9,281 earmarks worth \$10.2 billion in FY2010, down 17% by number and 19% by value (**Table 6**).

INTRODUCTION

During 2007, both the House and the Senate established new earmark transparency procedures for their respective chambers. They provide for public disclosure of approved earmarks and the identification of their congressional sponsors, among other requirements. These procedures currently are contained in House Rule XXI, clause 9, and Senate Rule XLIV.[1]

While the House rule requires disclosure of "congressional earmarks" and the Senate rule requires disclosure of "congressionally directed spending items," the terms are defined in the same way. Thus, this report uses the term "earmark" to encompass both a "congressional earmark" as used in the House rule and a "congressionally directed spending item" as used in the Senate rule. Under both chambers' rules, an earmark is a provision in legislation or report language that meets certain criteria. First, it is included primarily at the request of a Member. Second, it provides, authorizes, or recommends a specific amount of discretionary budget authority, credit authority, or other spending authority (1) to an entity, or (2) to a specific state, locality, or congressional district. However, the rules exclude funding set-asides that are selected through a statutory or administrative formula-driven or competitive award process.[2]

This report provides information on the earmarks disclosed by the House and Senate for the 12 regular, annual appropriations bills for each of FY2008, FY2009, and FY20 10. For these bills, a list of earmarks was typically included in the explanatory statement accompanying the final version of the bill, under the heading "Disclosure of Earmarks and Congressionally Directed Spending Items."[3] The abbreviations in **Table 1** are used to reference the bills.

The appropriations committees began publishing these disclosure lists in FY2008, the first year under the new rules. This report analyzes the data in the lists directly, without additions or deletions, as explained below. The disclosures typically identify the federal agency, project name, amount, and requester. In some cases, other information also has been included, such as an account within an agency, or the recipient, purpose, or location of the earmark.

For FY2008-FY2010, the explanatory statement for the State-Foreign Operations appropriations bill states that neither the bill text nor the accompanying explanatory statement contain earmarks as defined in House and Senate rules. Consequently, most of the discussion in this report focuses on the other 11 appropriations bills, for which Congress disclosed earmarks for each fiscal year.

Table 1. Appropriations Bills

Appropriations Bill	Abbreviation
Agriculture, Rural Development, Food and Drug Administration, and Related Agencies	Agriculture
Commerce, Justice, Science, and Related Agencies	Commerce-Justice-Science
Defense	Defense
Energy and Water Development and Related Agencies	Energy-Water
Financial Services and General Government	Financial Services
Homeland Security	Homeland Security
Interior, Environment, and Related Agencies	Interior-Environment
Labor, Health and Human Services, and Education, and Related Agencies	Labor-HHS-Education
Legislative Branch	Legislative Branch
Military Construction and Veterans Affairs and Related Agencies	Military Construction-VA
State, Foreign Operations, and Related Programs	State-Foreign Operations
Transportation, Housing and Urban Development, and Related Agencies	Transportation-HUD

Source: CRS.

This report does not address earmarks disclosed for bills other than the 12 regular, annual appropriations bills for FY2008-FY2010. For example, it does not pertain to any earmarks disclosed for supplemental appropriations bills or for authorizing legislation.

Tabulations in this report reflect all earmarks in the FY2008-FY2010 disclosure lists for the 11 appropriations bills, regardless of what information is provided for each entry. For instance, no distinctions are drawn based on the indicated requester. Some of the items identify the requester as one or more Members, others note only the President, while still others indicate the President and Members.[4] Similarly, the counts of earmarks include those items in the disclosure lists for which no funding level was indicated.

Observers of the budget process frequently focus on earmarks that were originated by Congress. However, earmarking is not solely a congressional activity. Observers also have identified earmarking conducted by the President and others in the executive branch during budget formulation and execution, both at their discretion and through interactions with Congress.[5] There is no source that defines and comprehensively identifies executive branch earmarks. Nevertheless, some of the FY2008-FY20 10 congressional disclosure lists identify earmarks as requested solely by the President, or by the President and one or more Members. A discussion of these earmarks disclosed for FY20 10 is presented below in the section on "Congressionally Disclosed Earmarks Requested by the President," and for FY2008-FY20 10 in the section on "Recent Earmark Trends: FY2008 to FY2010."

The tabulations in this report reflect the value of the earmarks in the disclosure lists, although subsequent actions could have altered them. For instance, rescissions of funds might have reduced the amounts identified as earmarked. Additionally, some of the earmarks may not have been provided to recipients who did not comply with conditions or requirements.[6]

The balance of this report provides data on the earmarks disclosed by Congress for the FY2008- FY2010 regular annual appropriations bills. First, a series of tables and graphs depicts data for FY2010, the most recent fiscal year for which data are available for all enacted appropriations bills. Second, another series of tables and graphs compares earmarks for FY2010 with earmarks for prior years back to FY2008, the first year for which Congress published earmark disclosure lists under chamber rules. The tables and graphs contain data on the number and dollar value of the earmarks disclosed for each appropriations bill. They also identify the portion of each bill's total appropriation and non-mandatory funding that was earmarked.

DATA ON CONGRESSIONAL DISCLOSURE OF EARMARKS

Distribution of Earmarks in FY2010

In FY20 10, Congress identified 11,320 earmarks worth $32.0 billion. About 1.5% of the total regular FY20 10 appropriation was earmarked, 2.4% if mandatory appropriations are excluded (**Table 2**).

Table 2. FY2010 Earmarks Disclosed by Congress: Number, Dollar Value, and Percentage of Total and Non-Mandatory Appropriations, by Appropriations Bill

Appropriations Bill	Earmarks		Total appropriation in bill		Non-mandatory appropriation	
	Number	$ million	$ million	% earmarks	$ million	% earmarks
Energy-Water	2,293	5,728	33,978	16.9%	33,978	16.9%
Labor-HHS-Education	1,795	1,057	748,724[a]	0.1%	165,845[a]	0.6%
Defense	1,719	4,197	636,665	0.7%	636,374	0.7%
Transportation-HUD	1,576	3,071	122,143	2.5%	122,143	2.5%
Commerce-Justice-Science	1,513	781	68,174	1.1%	67,952	1.1%
Military Construction-VA	745	14,525	182,750	7.9%	126,182	11.5%
Interior-Environment	733	710	32,295	2.2%	32,240	2.2%
Agriculture	462	355	121,230	0.3%	23,401	1.5%
Financial Services	291	1,109	46,265	2.4%	25,696	4.3%
Homeland Security	192	420	44,137	1.0%	42,776	1.0%
Legislative Branch	1	0.20	4,656	0.004%	4,656	0.004%
State-Foreign Operations	0	0	48,923	0%	48,764	0%
Total	**11,320**	**31,954**	**2,089,941**	**1.5%**	**1,330,006**	**2.4%**

Source: CRS, compiled from appropriations totals in detailed funding tables and statements of "Disclosure of Earmarks and Congressionally Directed Spending Items" for P.L. 111-68, P.L. 111-80, P.L. 111-83, P.L. 111-85, P.L. 111-88, P.L. 111-117, and P.L. 111-118.

Notes: Appropriations bills are ordered by the number of earmarks.

a. These totals do not include $831.0 million in previously appropriated FY20 10 funds for Pell Grants.

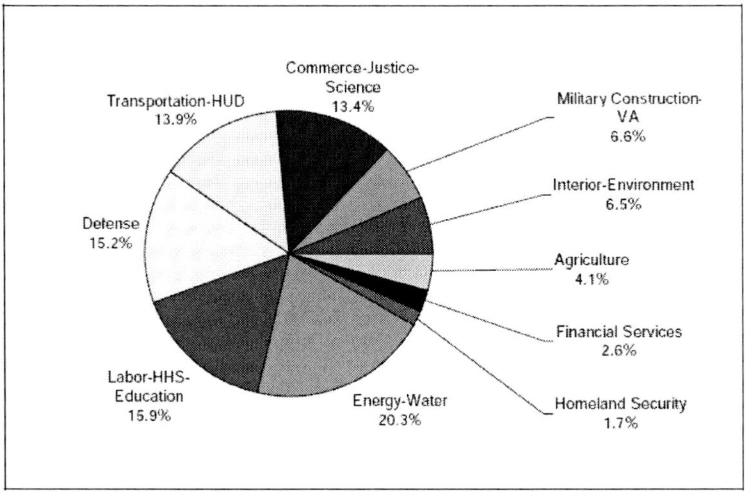

Source: CRS, compiled from the "Disclosure of Earmarks and Congressionally Directed Spending Items" for P.L. 111-68, P.L. 111-80, P.L. 111-83, P.L. 111-85, P.L. 111-88, P.L. 111-117, and P.L. 111-118.

Notes: Does not show the Legislative Branch bill (0.01%) or State-Foreign Operations (0%).

Figure 1. Distribution of Number of Earmarks by Appropriations Bill, FY2010 (Total: 11,320 earmarks in congressional disclosure lists).

Some appropriations bills account for more earmarks than others. About four-fifths (79%) of the 11,320 earmarks in FY20 10 are in five of the 12 appropriations bills (8,896 earmarks in Energy- Water, Labor-HHS-Education, Defense, Transportation-HUD, and Commerce-Justice-Science).

The Energy-Water bill contains the greatest number of FY20 10 earmarks (2,293, about 20% of all earmarks; **Figure 1**).

The distribution of the value of earmarks is more concentrated, with about $27.5 billion, or 86%, of the value of earmarks in four of the appropriations bills (Military Construction-VA, Energy- Water, Defense, and Transportation-HUD). The Military Construction-VA bill contains the greatest value of FY20 10 earmarks ($14.5 billion, about 45% of the combined value of earmarks; **Figure 2**).

Some appropriations bills account for fewer earmarks but have a greater share of the value, or vice versa. For example, Military Construction-VA is ranked sixth in the number of earmarks (with 7%), but is ranked first by the value of earmarks (with 45%). In contrast, five bills are ranked lower by the value of earmarks than their rank by number. Energy-Water is ranked first by number but second by value; Labor-HHS-Education is ranked second by number but sixth by value; Commerce-Justice-Science is ranked fifth by number but seventh by value; Interior is seventh by number but eighth by value, and Agriculture is eighth by number but tenth by value (**Figure 1** and **Figure 2**).

Earmarks as a Percentage of Appropriations in FY2010

Another measure of the magnitude of earmarks is the percentage of the appropriation that is earmarked. There are various types of appropriations totals, but perhaps the two most relevant for this comparison are the grand total and the total of non-mandatory appropriations (**Table 2**).

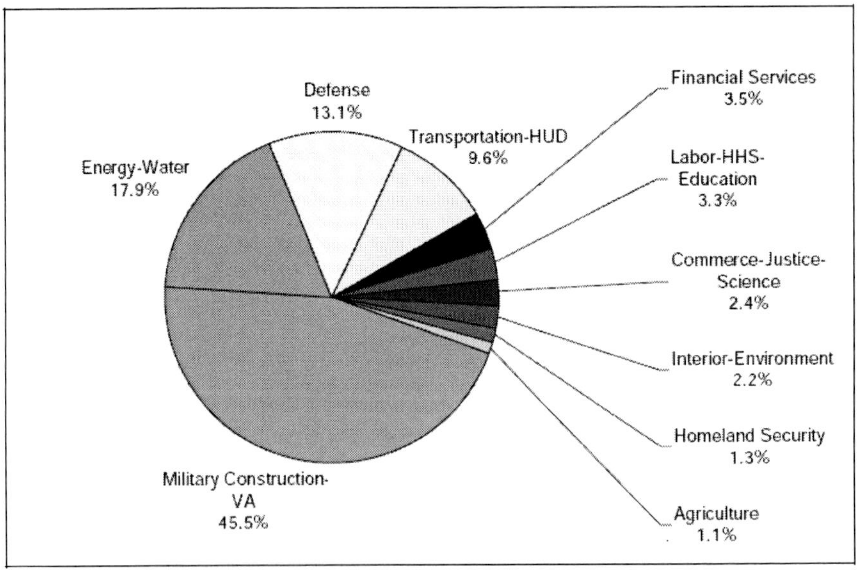

Source: CRS, compiled from the "Disclosure of Earmarks and Congressionally Directed Spending Items" for P.L. 111-68, P.L. 111-80, P.L. 111-83, P.L. 111-85, P.L. 111-88, P.L. 111-1 17, and P.L. 111-118.

Notes: Does not show the Legislative Branch bill (0.001%) or State-Foreign Operations (0%).

Figure 2. Distribution of Value of Earmarks by Appropriations Bill, FY2010 (Total: $32.0 billion in congressional disclosure lists).

Earmarks are predominantly, if not exclusively, found in discretionary accounts. All appropriations bills include discretionary spending, and some include mandatory spending. Discretionary spending supports a wide variety of activities. It is controlled by the appropriations acts, which are under the jurisdiction of the House and Senate Committees on Appropriations. Mandatory spending primarily funds entitlement programs. It is controlled by the authorization (or legislative) acts, which are under the jurisdiction of the authorizing committees.[7]

In addition, the Transportation-HUD bill separately identifies contract authority, which is included in these tables as non-mandatory appropriations. The difference between the total and non-mandatory appropriations can be large for some bills, such as Labor-HHS-Education (which has mandatory funds for Medicare and Medicaid, among other programs) and Agriculture (which has mandatory funds for food stamps and the farm commodity programs).

For all 12 FY20 10 appropriations bills combined, 1.5% of the total value of regular appropriation is earmarked, and 2.4% of the non-mandatory appropriation is earmarked.

The percentages of regular FY2010 total appropriations that were earmarked ranged from 0% for the State-Foreign Operations appropriations bill to 16.9% for the Energy-Water appropriations bill (**Table 2, Figure 3**). However, for all of the bills except two (Energy-Water, and Military Construction-VA), the percentages of total appropriations that were earmarked are less than 3%.

When mandatory funds are excluded, the percentages earmarked can change significantly. For example, the percentage of the FY20 10 total appropriation earmarked for Military Construction- VA is 7.9%, but it increases to 11.5% of the non-mandatory appropriation (Table 2, Figure 3). For Financial Services, the respective percentages are 2.4% and 4.3%; for Agriculture, 0.3% and 1.5%; and for Labor-HHS-Education, 0.1% and 0.6%.

Congressionally Disclosed Earmarks Requested by the President

House and Senate rules do not require congressional disclosure of presidentially requested earmarks. The disclosure lists for some bills, however, include the "President" as a requester. **Table 3** presents the number and value of FY20 10 earmarks in the disclosure lists that were requested by the President. It is not clear that Administration earmarks are defined or disclosed consistently across all appropriations bills. Thus, it is possible that there may be more presidentially requested earmarks than are reflected in **Table 3**. The disclosure list for the FY20 10 Financial Services bill also identified the Judiciary as a requester for five earmarks.

Nine of the 11 FY2010 appropriations bills with congressionally disclosed earmarks list the "President" (or the "Judiciary") as a requester of some earmarks, alone or with Members of Congress. The total across all appropriations bills in FY20 10 is 2,039 earmarks worth $21.8 billion (18% of the total number and 68% of the total value). Only the Defense and Legislative Branch appropriations bills did not identify earmarks as requested by the President in FY2010.

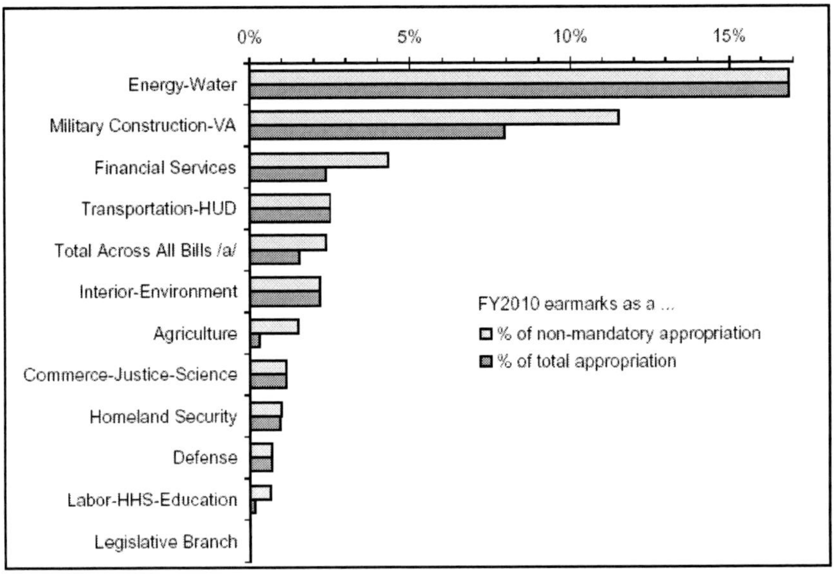

Source: CRS, compiled from appropriations totals in detailed funding tables and statements of "Disclosure of Earmarks and Congressionally Directed Spending Items" for P.L. 111-68, P.L. 111-80, P.L. 111-83, P.L. 111-85, P.L. 111-88, P.L. 111-117, and P.L. 111-118.

Notes: Appropriations bills are ordered by the percentage of non-mandatory appropriations that is earmarked. This figure does not show the State-Foreign Operations bill because it had no earmarks.

/a/ Reflects the percentages of the non-mandatory and total appropriations that were earmarked across all 1 2 bills (2.4% and 1.5%, respectively).

Figure 3. Earmark Values as a Percentage of Non-Mandatory and Total Appropriations by Bill, FY2010.

- The President is disclosed as the only requester (no Members of Congress are listed) for a subset of earmarks. The 12-bill total is 1,265 earmarks worth $9.5 billion (11% of the 11,320 total number and 30% of the $32.0 billion total value). The Energy-Water bill had 768 of these earmarks worth $2.0 billion; Military Construction-VA is next with 320 earmarks for $6.4 billion (**Figure 4, Figure 5**).
- The President (or the Judiciary) and Members of Congress jointly requested another subset of earmarks. The 12-bill total is 774 earmarks worth $12.4 billion (7% of the 11,320 total number and 39% of the $32.0 billion total value). The Energy-Water bill has 409 of these earmarks worth $2.7 billion, and the Military Construction-VA bill had 243 earmarks worth $7.0 billion (**Figure 4, Figure 5**).

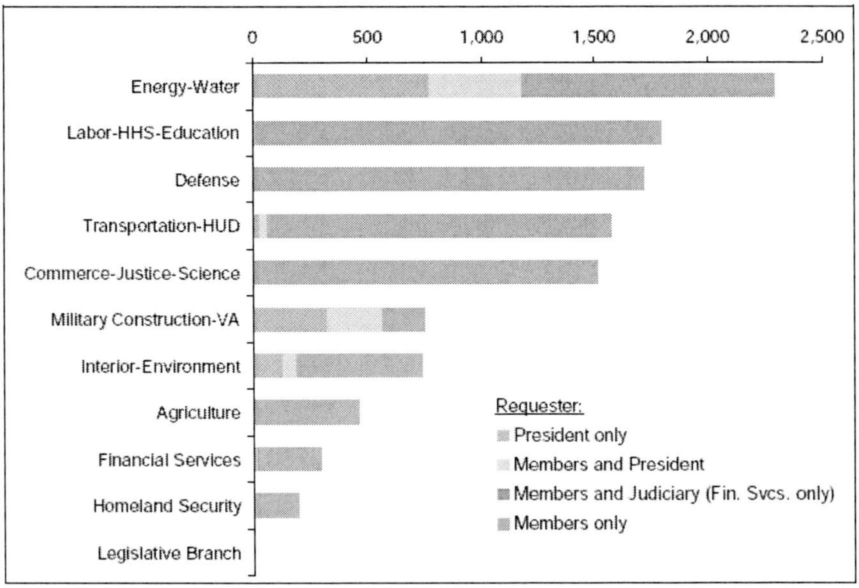

Source: CRS, compiled from earmark disclosure lists for enacted appropriations acts.

Notes: Appropriations bills are ordered by the total number of earmarks. This figure does not show the State- Foreign Operations bill because it had no earmarks.

Figure 4. Number of Congressionally Disclosed Earmarks That Were Requested by the President, the Judiciary, and Members of Congress, FY2010.

Table 3. Congressionally Disclosed Earmarks That Were Requested by the President and Members of Congress, FY2010

Bill	Number				Value ($ million)			
	President only	Members and President	Members only	Total	President only	Members and President	Members only	Total
Energy-Water	768	409	1,116	2,293	1,988	2,711	1,028	5,728
Labor-HHS-Education	1	11	1,783	1,795	11	167	879	1,057
Defense	0	0	1,719	1,719	0	0	4,197	4,197
Transportation-HUD	31	29	1,516	1,576	275	1,586	1,210	3,071
Commerce-Justice-Science	2	0	1,511	1,513	67	0	715	781
Military Construction-VA	320	243	182	745	6,379	7,046	1,100	14,525
Interior-Environment	129	62	542	733	212	158	341	710
Agriculture	1	2	459	462	1	3	351	355
Financial Services	10	10[a]	271	291	506	538[a]	65	1,109
Homeland Security	3	8	181	192	12	144	264	420
Legislative Branch	0	0	1	1	0	0	0.20	0.20
State-Foreign Operations	0	0	0	0	0	0	0	0
Total	**1,265**	**774**	**9,281**	**11,320**	**9,450**	**12,353**	**10,151**	**31,954**

Source: CRS, compiled from the "Disclosure of Earmarks and Congressionally Directed Spending Items" for P.L. 111-68, P.L. 111-80, P.L. 111-83, P.L. 111-85, P.L. 111-88, P.L. 111-117, and P.L. 111-118.

Notes: Appropriations bills are ordered by the total number of earmarks.

a. Contains five earmarks totaling $282.9 million that were requested jointly by Members and the Judiciary. FY20 10 is the first year that the disclosure lists include earmarks by the Judiciary. These earmarks support U.S. Courthouse projects through the General Services Administration (GSA).

The final subset of earmarks are those requested solely by Members of Congress. The total across all appropriations bills in FY20 10 is 9,281 earmarks worth $10.2 billion (82% of the 11,320 total number and 32% of the $32.0 billion total value; **Table 3**). The Labor-HHS-Education, Defense, Transportation-HUD, and Commerce-Justice-Science appropriations bills each had between 1,500 and 1,800 Member-only earmarks (**Figure 4**). Among these, Defense accounted for $4.2 billion of the earmarks, followed next by Transportation-HUD with $1.2 billion of Member-only earmarks (**Figure 5**).

As implied above, the vast majority of earmarks (82%) are Member-only earmarks, while the value of earmarks is more evenly split among the three categories of requesters. Specifically, the earmarks requested jointly by the President and Members accounted for 39% of the total earmark value, followed by Member-only requests with 32% of the value and President-only requests at 30% of the value.

The relatively large number and dollar value of presidentially requested earmarks for Military Construction-VA and Energy-Water reflect the practices of some agencies within these bills of requesting and managing funds at the project level. Specifically, the Department of Defensetypically requests funds for individual military construction projects, and such requests are among those disclosed for the Military Construction-VA bill. Similarly, the Corps of Engineers and the Bureau of Reclamation typically request funds for specific agency projects, and these requests are among the earmarks disclosed for the Energy-Water bill.

Recent Earmark Trends: FY2008 to FY2010

From FY2008 to FY2010, the three years with disclosure lists, the number of appropriations earmarks decreased 12% to 11,320 (1,490 fewer earmarks). However, the value increased 11% to $32.0 billion (+$3. 1 billion, **Table 4**). Over the same period, total appropriations increased by 31%. Thus, the percentage of the appropriations that was earmarked decreased in FY20 10: 1.5% of the total appropriation (down from 1.8% in both FY2008 and FY2009) and 2.4% of the non- mandatory appropriation (down from 2.9% in both FY2008 and FY2009, **Table 5**).

Table 4. FY2008 and FY2010 Earmarks Disclosed by Congress: Number and Dollar Value, by Appropriations Bill

Appropriations bill	Number				Value ($ million)			
	FY2008	FY20 10	Change	% Change	FY2008	FY20 10	Change	% Change
Energy-Water	2,427	2,293	-134	-6%	6,595	5,728	-868	- 13%
Labor-HHS-Education	2,241	1,795	-446	-20%	1,027	1,057	+30	+3%
Defense	2,049	1,719	-330	-16%	4,982	4,197	-785	-16%
Transportation-HUD	2,149	1,576	-573	-27%	2,954	3,071	+117	+4%
Commerce-Justice-Science	1,728	1,513	-215	-12%	823	781	-42	-5%
Military Construction-VA	573	745	+172	+30%	10,044	14,525	+4,481	+45%
Interior-Environment	651	733	+82	+13%	625	710	+86	+14%
Agriculture	623	462	-161	-26%	402	355	-47	-12%
Financial Services	234	291	+57	+24%	1,001	1,109	+ 107	+ 11%
Homeland Security	131	192	+61	+47%	424	420	-3	- 1%
Legislative Branch	4	1	-3	-75%	0.40	0.20	-0.20	-50%
State-Foreign Operations	0	0	0	0%	0	0	0	0%
Total	**12,810**	**11,320**	**-1,490**	**-12%**	**28,878**	**31,954**	**+3,076**	**+11%**

Source: CRS, compiled from the statements of "Disclosure of Earmarks and Congressionally Directed Spending Items" for FY2008 (P.L. 110-116, P.L. 110-161) and FY2010 (P.L. 111-68, P.L. 111-80, P.L. 111-83, P.L. 111-85, P.L. 111-88, P.L. 111-117, and P.L. 111-118).

Notes: Bills are ordered by the number of earmarks in FY20 10. Numbers may not add due to rounding.

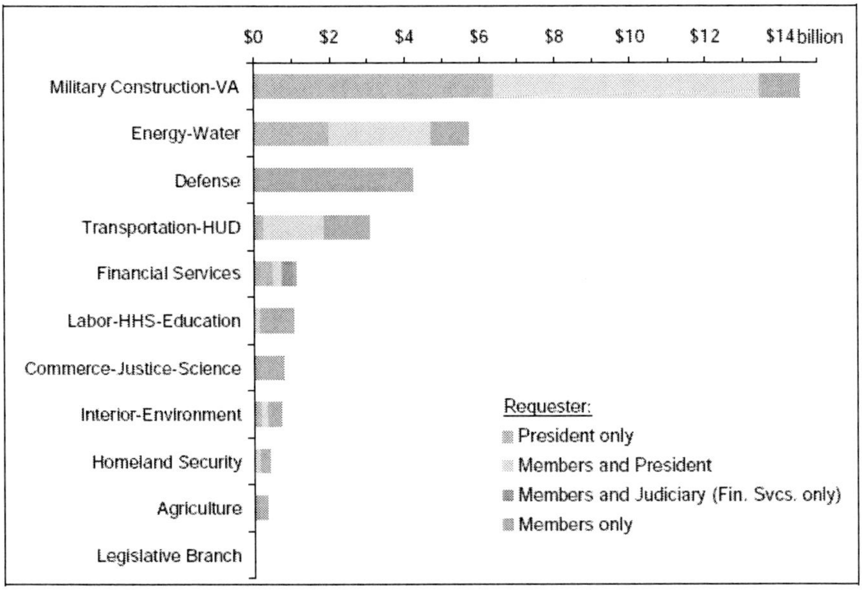

Source: CRS, compiled from earmark disclosure lists for enacted appropriations acts.

Notes: Appropriations bills are ordered by the total value of earmarks. This figure does not show the State- Foreign Operations bill because it had no earmarks.

Figure 5. Value of Congressionally Disclosed Earmarks That Were Requested by the President, the Judiciary, and Members of Congress, FY2010.

Seven of the 11 bills with earmarks had a decrease in number, including the five bills accounting for 79% of the earmarks (Energy-Water, Labor-HHS-Education, Defense, Transportation-HUD, and Commerce-Justice-Science; **Figure 6**). Two of these bills (Transportation-HUD and LaborHHS-Education) accounted for 68% of the decline in number (1,019 fewer earmarks). Four bills (Military Construction-VA, Interior-Environment, Homeland Security, and Financial Services) had an increase in the number (372 more earmarks).

Six of 11 bills had a decrease in the value of earmarks, subtotaling a $1.7 billion decline. Five bills (Military Construction-VA, Transportation-HUD, Financial Services, Interior-Environment, and Labor-HHS-Education) had an increase in the value of earmarks. The Military Construction- VA bill accounts for the magnitude of the increase in the value of earmarks, with a $4.5 billion (+45%) increase over two years (**Figure 7**). Excluding Military Construction-VA, the value of earmarks for the remaining bills is down 7% (-$1.4 billion) in the two years since FY2008.

Table 5. FY2008-FY2010 Earmarks Disclosed by Congress: Number, Dollar Value, and Percentage of Total and Non-Mandatory Appropriations, by Appropriations Bill

Bill and year	Earmarks		Total appropriation in bill		Non-mandatory appropriation	
	Number	$ million	$ million	% earmarks	$ million	% earmarks
Energy-Water						
FY2008	2,427	6,595	31,466[a]	21.0%[b]	31,466[a]	21.0%[b]
FY2009	2,403	5,940	33,795	17.6%	33,795	17.6%
FY2010	2,293	5,728	33,978	16.9%	33,978	16.9%
Military Construction-VA						
FY2008	573	10,044	108,391	9.3%	63,904	15.7%
FY2009	578	12,213	119,608	10.2%	72,865	16.8%
FY2010	745	14,525	182,750	7.9%	126,182	11.5%
Financial Services						
FY2008	234	1,001	43,281	2.3%	20,599	4.9%
FY2009	279	1,153	44,582	2.6%	22,697	5.1%
FY2010	291	1,109	46,265	2.4%	25,696	4.3%
Transportation-HUD						
FY2008	2,149	2,954	103,579	2.9%	103,579[c]	2.9%
FY2009	1,879	3,084	109,063	2.8%	109,063[c]	2.8%
FY2010	1,576	3,071	122,143	2.5%	122,143	2.5%
Interior-Environment						
FY2008	651	625	26,891[a]	2.3%[b]	26,831[a,c]	2.3%[b]

Table 5. (Continued)

Bill and year	Earmarks		Total appropriation in bill		Non-mandatory appropriation	
	Number	$ million	$ million	% earmarks	$ million	% earmarks
FY2009	562	554	27,591	2.0%	27,579	2.0%
FY2010	733	710	32,295	2.2%	32,240	2.2%
Agriculture						
FY2008	623	402	91,028[a]	0.4%[b]	19,527[a]	2.1%[b]
FY2009	521	380	107,682[d]	0.4%	21,053[d]	1.8%
FY2010	462	355	121,230	0.3%	23,401	1.5%
Commerce-Justice-Science						
FY2008	1,728	823	53,735	1.5%	53,507[c]	1.5%
FY2009	1,545	758	59,845[e]	1.3%	59,624[c,e]	1.3%
FY2010	1,513	781	68,174	1.1%	67,952[c]	1.1%
Homeland Security						
FY2008	131	424	38,747	1.1%	37,562	1.1%
FY2009	149	738	41,225	1.8%	39,989	1.8%
FY2010	192	420	44,137	1.0%	42,776	1.0%
Defense[f]						
FY2008	2,049	4,982	459,594	1.1%	459,332	1.1%
FY2009	2,025	4,866	488,016	1.0%	487,737	1.0%
FY2010	1,719	4,197	636,665	0.7%	636,374	0.7%
Labor-HHS-Education						
FY2008	2,241	1,027	603,91 7[a]	0.2%[b]	1 48,652[a]	0.7%[b]

Table 5. (Continued)

Bill and year	Earmarks		Total appropriation in bill		Non-mandatory appropriation	
	Number	$ million	$ million	% earmarks	$ million	% earmarks
FY2009	2,155	973	633,367[g]	0.2%	154,977[g]	0.6%
FY2010	1,795	1,057	748,724[h]	0.1%	1 65,845[h]	0.6%
Legislative Branch						
FY2008	4	0.40	3,970[a]	0.01 0%[b]	3,970[a]	0.01 0%[b]
FY2009	3	0.38	4,402	0.009%	4,402	0.009%
FY2010	1	0.20	4,656	0.004%	4,656	0.004%
State-Foreign Operations						
FY2008	0	0	35,343[a]	0%	35,1 84[a]	0%
FY2009	0	0	36,777[i]	0%	36,620[i]	0%
FY20 10	0	0	48,923	0%	48,764	0%
Total						
FY2008	**12,810**	**28,878**	**1,599,941**	**1.8%**	**1,004,111**	**2.9%**
FY2009	**12,099**	**30,661**	**1,705,953**	**1.8%**	**1,070,401**	**2.9%**
FY2010	**11,320**	**31,954**	**2,089,941**	**1.5%**	**1,330,006**	**2.4%**

Source: CRS, compiled from appropriations totals in detailed funding tables and statements of "Disclosure of Earmarks and Congressionally Directed Spending Items" for FY2008 (P.L. 110-116, P.L. 110-161), FY2009 (P.L. 110-329, P.L. 111-8), and FY2010 (P.L. 111-68, P.L. 111-80, P.L. 111-83, P.L. 111-85, P.L. 111-88, P.L. 111-117, and P.L. 111-118).

Notes: Appropriations bills are ordered by the FY20 10 earmark value as a percentage of non-mandatory appropriations.

a. This figure reflects an across-the-board reduction as detailed in P.L. 110-161. The percentage of the reduction varies for different bills, but ranges from 0.25% for Legislative Branch to 0.7% for Agriculture, 0.8 1% for State-Foreign Operations, 1.6% and 0.9 1% for Energy-Water, 1.56% for Interior-Environment, and 1.747% for Labor-H H S-Education.

b. The dollar value of earmarks in the disclosure list *without* the across-the-board reduction is compared to the total appropriation and non-mandatory appropriation *with* the across-the-board reduction. However, this inconsistency does not appear to materially affect the percentages reported because the sizes of both the across-the-board cuts and the value of earmarks as a percentage of appropriations were relatively small.

c. The amount of mandatory appropriations was provided by the House Appropriations Committee.

d. These totals do not include $405.0 million in previously appropriated FY2009 supplemental funds that are included in the tables accompanying the FY2009 omnibus appropriations act.

e. These totals do not include $82.6 million in previously appropriated FY2009 supplemental funds that are included in the tables accompanying the FY2009 omnibus appropriations act.

f. Total appropriations and non-mandatory appropriations reflect scorekeeping adjustments.

g. These totals do not include $5.1 billion in previously appropriated FY2009 funds for the Low-Income Home Energy Assistance Program (LIHEAP).

h. These totals do not include $831.0 million in previously appropriated FY2010 funds for Pell Grants.

i. These totals do not include $3.68 billion in previously appropriated FY2009 supplemental funds that are included in the tables accompanying the FY2009 omnibus appropriations act.

Table 6. Congressionally Disclosed Earmarks That Were Requested by the President and Members of Congress, FY2008- FY2010

Bill, year	Number							Value						
	President only		Members and President		Members only		Total	President only		Members and President		Members only		Total
	Nbr.	% of total	Nbr.	% of total	Nbr.	% of total		Value ($ mil.)	% of total	Value ($ mil.)	% of total	Value ($ mil.)	% of total	
Energy-Water														
FY2008	680	28%	467	19%	1,280	53%	**2,427**	1,679	25%	3,389	51%	1,527	23%	**6,595**
FY2009	565	24%	646	27%	1,192	50%	**2,403**	1,040	18%	3,578	60%	1,321	22%	**5,940**

Table 6. (Continued)

Bill, year	Number							Value						
	President only		Members and President		Members only		Total	President only		Members and President		Members only		Total
	Nbr.	% of total	Nbr.	% of total	Nbr.	% of total		Value ($ mil.)	% of total	Value ($ mil.)	% of total	Value ($ mil.)	% of total	
FY2010	768	33%	409	18%	1,116	49%	**2,293**	1,988	35%	2,711	47%	1,028	18%	**5,728**
Labor-HHS-Education														
FY2008	0	0%	0	0%	2,241	100%	**2,241**	0	0%	0	0%	1,027	100%	**1,027**
FY2009	0	0%	0	0%	2,155	100%	**2,155**	0	0%	0	0%	973	100%	**973**
FY2010	1	0.1%	11	1%	1,783	99%	**1,795**	11	1%	167	16%	879	83%	**1,057**
Defense														
FY2008	0	0%	0	0%	2,049	100%	**2,049**	0	0%	0	0%	4,982	100%	**4,982**
FY2009	0	0%	0	0%	2,025	100%	**2,025**	0	0%	0	0%	4,866	100%	**4,866**
FY2010	0	0%	0	0%	1,719	100%	**1,719**	0	0%	0	0%	4,197	100%	**4,197**
Transportation-HUD														
FY2008	13	1%	27	1%	2,109	98%	**2,149**	128	4%	1,181	40%	1,645	56%	**2,954**
FY2009	13	1%	33	2%	1,833	98%	**1,879**	108	4%	1,489	48%	1,487	48%	**3,084**
FY2010	31	2%	29	2%	1,516	96%	**1,576**	275	9%	1,586	52%	1,210	39%	**3,071**
Commerce-Justice-Science														
FY2008	0	0%	0	0%	1,728	100%	**1,728**	0	0%	0	0%	823	100%	**823**
FY2009	0	0%	0	0%	1,545	100%	**1,545**	0	0%	0	0%	758	100%	**758**
FY2010	2	0.1%	0	0%	1,511	99.9%	**1,513**	67	9%	0	0%	715	91%	**781**
Military Construction-VA														
FY2008	126	22%	256	45%	191	33%	**573**	2,379	24%	6,484	65%	1,181	12%	**10,044**
FY2009	110	19%	291	50%	177	31%	**578**	2,666	22%	8,225	67%	1,323	11%	**12,213**
FY2010	320	43%	243	33%	182	24%	**745**	6,379	44%	7,046	49%	1,100	8%	**14,525**
Interior-Environment														
FY2008	0	0%	95	15%	556	85%	**651**	0	0%	215	34%	410	66%	**625**

Table 6. (Continued)

Bill, year	Number							Value						
	President only		Members and President		Members only		Total	President only		Members and President		Members only		Total
	Nbr.	% of total	Nbr.	% of total	Nbr.	% of total		Value ($ mil.)	% of total	Value ($ mil.)	% of total	Value ($ mil.)	% of total	
FY2009	0	0%	19	3%	543	97%	**562**	0	0%	121	22%	434	78%	**554**
FY2010	129	18%	62	8%	542	74%	**733**	212	30%	158	22%	341	48%	**710**
Agriculture														
FY2008	0	0%	10	2%	613	98%	**623**	0	0%	12	3%	391	97%	**402**
FY2009	0	0%	4	1%	517	99%	**521**	0	0%	4	1%	375	99%	**380**
FY2010	1	0.2%	2	0.4%	459	99%	**462**	1	0.4%	3	1%	351	99%	**355**
Financial Services														
FY2008	0	0%	14	6%	220	94%	**234**	0	0%	755	75%	247	25%	**1,001**
FY2009	9	3%	4	1%	266	95%	**279**	667	58%	343	30%	142	12%	**1,153**
FY2010	10	3%	10 a	3%	271	93%	**291**	506	46%	538 a	48%	65	6%	**1,109**
Homeland Security														
FY2008	0	0%	5	4%	126	96%	**13 1**	0	0%	182	43%	242	57%	**424**
FY2009	23	15%	4	3%	122	82%	**149**	312	42%	93	13%	333	45%	**738**
FY2010	3	2%	8	4%	181	94%	**192**	12	3%	144	34%	264	63%	**420**
Legislative Branch														
FY2008	0	0%	0	0%	4	100%	**4**	0	0%	0	0%	0.40	100%	**0.40**
FY2009	0	0%	0	0%	3	100%	**3**	0	0%	0	0%	0.38	100%	**0.38**
FY2010	0	0%	0	0%	1	100%	**1**	0	0%	0	0%	0.20	100%	**0.20**
State-Foreign Operations														
FY2008	0	0%	0	0%	0	0%	**0**	0	0%	0	0%	0	0%	**0**
FY2009	0	0%	0	0%	0	0%	**0**	0	0%	0	0%	0	0%	**0**
FY2010	0	0%	0	0%	0	0%	**0**	0	0%	0	0%	0	0%	**0**

Table 6. (Continued)

Bill, year	Number							Value						
	President only		Members and President		Members only		Total	President only		Members and President		Members only		Total
	Nbr.	% of total	Nbr.	% of total	Nbr.	% of total		Value ($ mil.)	% of total	Value ($ mil.)	% of total	Value ($ mil.)	% of total	
Total														
FY2008	819	6%	874	7%	11,117	87%	12,810	4,185	14%	12,217	42%	12,476	43%	28,878
FY2009	720	6%	1,001	8%	10,378	86%	12,099	4,794	16%	13,854	45%	12,013	39%	30,661
FY2010	1,265	11%	774	7%	9,281	82%	11,320	9,450	30%	12,353	39%	10,151	32%	31,954

Source: CRS, compiled from the statements of "Disclosure of Earmarks and Congressionally Directed Spending Items" for FY2008 (P.L. 110-116, P.L. 110-161), FY2009 (P.L. 110-329, P.L. 111-8), and FY2010 (P.L. 111-68, P.L. 111-80, P.L. 111-83, P.L. 111-85, P.L. 111-88, P.L. 111-117, and P.L. 111-118).

Notes: Appropriations bills are ordered by the total number of earmarks in FY2010.

a. Contains 5 earmarks totaling $282.9 million that were requested jointly by Members and the Judiciary. FY20 10 is the first year that the disclosure lists include earmarks by the Judiciary. These earmarks support U.S. Courthouse projects through the General Services Administration (GSA). Additional courthouse projects are requested by the President and/or Members.

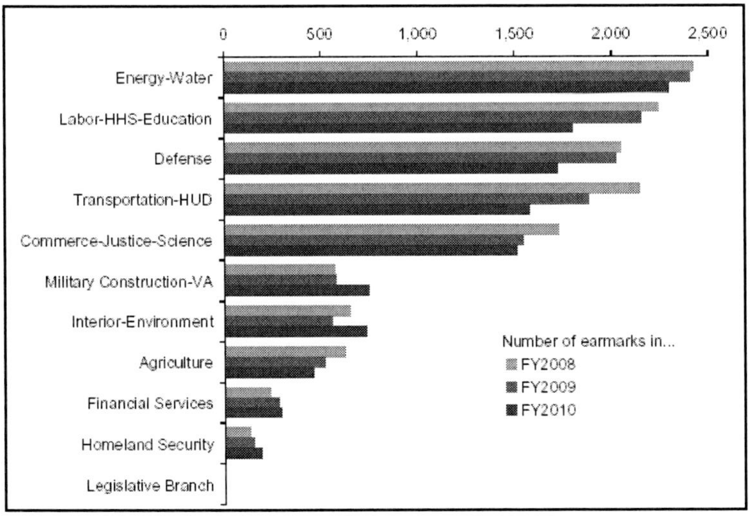

Source: CRS, compiled from earmark disclosure lists for enacted appropriations acts.

Notes: Appropriations bills are ordered by the number of earmarks in FY20 10. This figure does not show the State-Foreign Operations bill because it had no earmarks.

Figure 6. Number of Earmarks by Appropriations Bill, FY2008-FY2010.

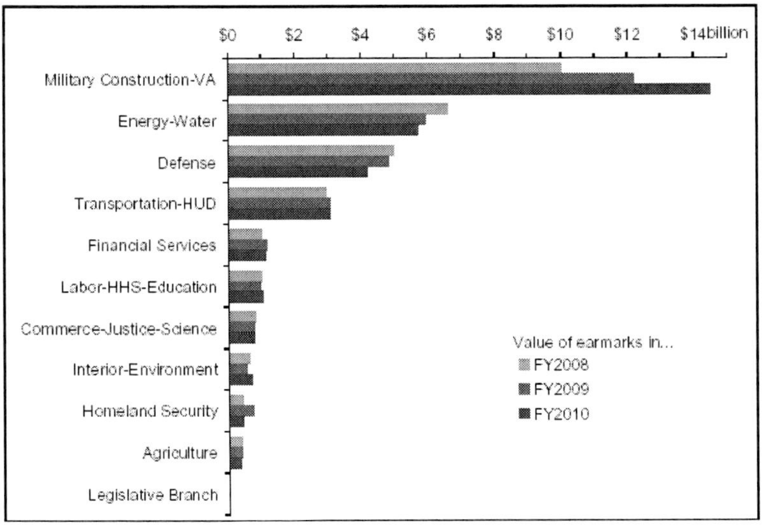

Source: CRS, compiled from earmark disclosure lists for enacted appropriations acts.

Notes: Appropriations bills are ordered by the value of earmarks in FY20 10. This figure does not show the State-Foreign Operations bill because it had no earmarks.

Figure 7. Value of Earmarks by Appropriations Bill, FY2008-FY2010.

Trends in Earmarks as a Percentage of Appropriations

Table 5 is a multi-year version of **Table 2** that contains data on the earmarked percentage of appropriations from FY2008 to FY2010, as well as the number and value of earmarks.

For each appropriations bill, the percentage of non-mandatory appropriations that was earmarked fell from FY2008 to FY2010 (**Figure 8**). This result occurred despite growth in the value of earmarks in some bills, as discussed earlier, because total appropriations increased by over 30%. For most bills the decline in the percentage earmarked was consistent over the three years, but for three bills the highest percentage was in the middle year. Over all 12 appropriations bills, the percentage of non-mandatory appropriations that was earmarked fell from 2.9% in FY2008 to 2.4% in FY20 10 (**Table 5**).

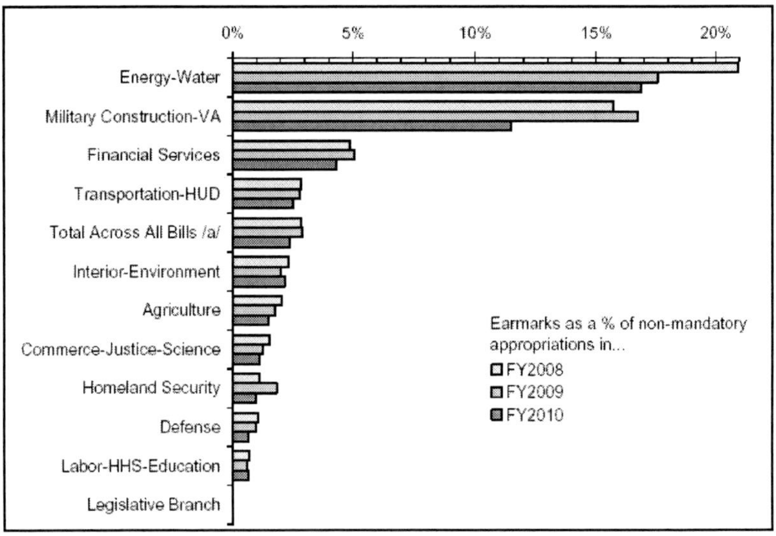

Source: CRS, compiled from appropriations totals and earmark disclosure lists for enacted appropriations acts.

Notes: Appropriations bills are ordered by the earmark value as a percentage of non-mandatory appropriations in FY20 10. This figure does not show the State-Foreign Operations bill because it had no earmarks.

/a/ Reflects the percentage of the total non-mandatory appropriation that was earmarked for all 12 bills (2.9% in FY2008 and FY2009, and 2.4% in FY20 10).

Figure 8. Earmark Values as a Percentage of Non-Mandatory Appropriations by Bill, FY2008- FY2010.

Trends in Congressionally Disclosed Earmarks Requested by the President

Table 6 is a multi-year version of **Table 3** that contains data on the number, value, and percentage of presidential earmarks in appropriations bills from FY2008 to FY2010. **Figure 9** and **Figure 10** are multi-year versions of the earlier figures (**Figure 4** and **Figure 5**) on presidential earmarks.

Both the number and value of earmarks requested solely by the President increased since FY2008. The number of such earmarks increased 54%, from 819 to 1,265, while the value increased 126%, from $4.2 billion to $9.5 billion. The increase in the number of President-only earmarks is counter to the decrease in the total number of earmarks over the FY2008-FY2010 period (discussed in **Table 4**). The 126% increase in the value of President-only earmarks notably exceeds the 11% increase in the total value of earmarks since FY2008.

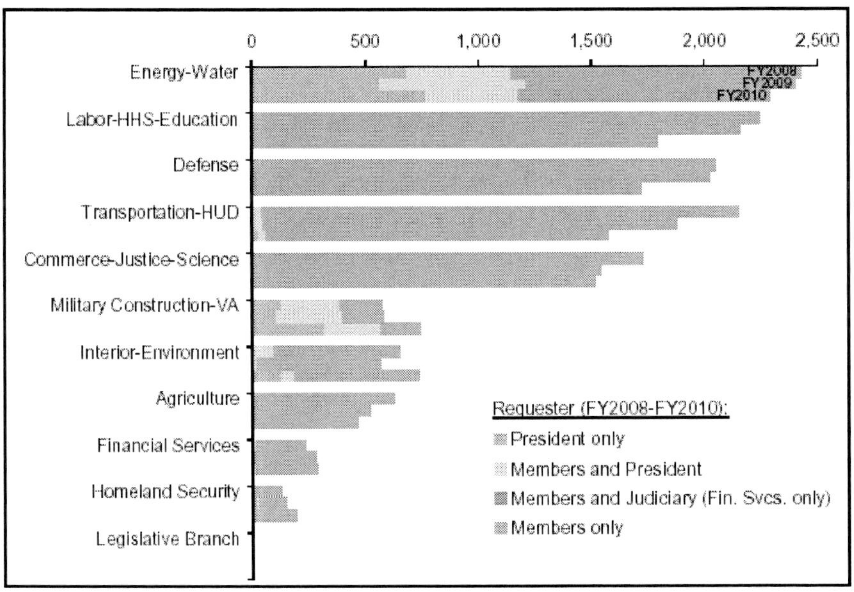

Source: CRS, compiled from earmark disclosure lists for enacted appropriations acts.

Notes: Appropriations bills are ordered by the total number of earmarks in FY2010. This figure does not show the State-Foreign Operations bill because it had no earmarks.

Figure 9. Number of Congressionally Disclosed Earmarks That Were Requested by the President, the Judiciary, and Members of Congress, FY2008-FY2010.

Conversely, the number and value of earmarks requested solely by Members have decreased, by 17% and 19% respectively, from 11,117 earmarks worth $12.5 billion in FY2008 to 9,281 earmarks worth $10.2 billion in FY20 10. This 17% decrease in the number of Member-only earmarks is a larger decrease than the 12% overall decrease in the number of earmarks from FY2008 to FY20 10 (**Table 4**). The 19% decrease in the value of Member-only earmarks is counter to the 11% increase in the total value of earmarks since FY2008.

The number and value of earmarks requested jointly by the President and Members of Congress were relatively more steady. The number of such earmarks fell 11% from 874 in FY2008 to 774 in FY20 10, while the value of those earmarks rose 1% from $12.2 billion to $12.4 billion.

Even if Military Construction-VA earmarks are excluded, the trends are still similar. For the rest of the appropriations bills excluding Military Construction, the total number of earmarks requested solely by the President increased 36%, while the number of Member-only earmarks decreased 17%. In terms of the value of earmarks, the total value of earmarks requested solely by the President increased 70%, while the value of Member-only earmarks decreased 20%.

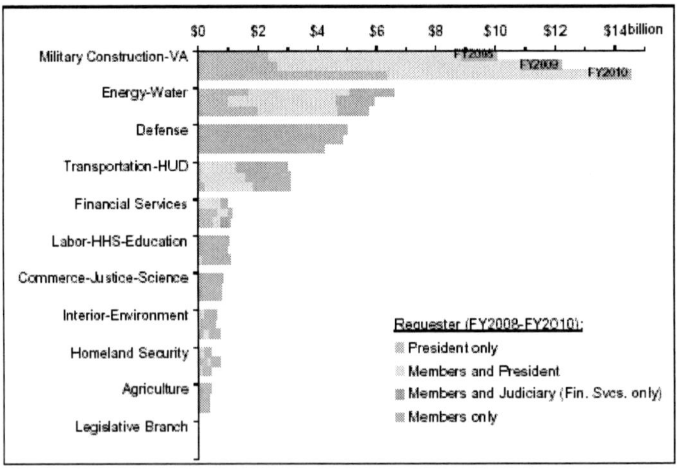

Source: CRS, compiled from earmark disclosure lists for enacted appropriations acts.

Notes: Appropriations bills are ordered by the total value of earmarks in FY2010. This figure does not show the State-Foreign Operations bill because it had no earmarks.

Figure 10. Value of Congressionally Disclosed Earmarks That Were Requested by the President, the Judiciary, and Members of Congress, FY2008-FY2010.

End Notes

1 House Rules are available at http://frwebgate.access1 10_cong_house_rules_manual&docid=1 10hruletx-78.pdf. Senate Rules are available at *http://frwebgate.access.gpo.gov/cgi-bin/getdoc.cgi?dbname=110_senate_ manual&docid=sd001_110-2.pdf.*

2 This report describes only selected provisions of the earmark disclosure rules. The summary here is derived from CRS Report RL34462, *House and Senate Procedural Rules Concerning Earmark Disclosure*, by Sandy Streeter. That report provides a fuller explanation and comparison of the earmark procedures and requirements in House and Senate rules.

For information on the disposition of points of order raised in the Senate under these rules, see CRS Report RS22733, *Senate Rules Restricting the Content of Conference Reports*, by Elizabeth Rybicki. Further, two CRS companion reports outline the major administrative responsibilities of Members and committees associated with the earmark disclosure rules. They are CRS Report RS22866, *Earmark Disclosure Rules in the House: Member and Committee Requirements*, by Megan Suzanne Lynch and CRS Report RS22867, *Earmark Disclosure Rules in the Senate: Member and Committee Requirements*, by Megan Suzanne Lynch.

3 In requiring disclosure of earmarks in appropriations acts or report language, House and Senate rules apply to earmarks in regular appropriations bills and each bill's accompanying conference report. Conference reports contain two parts. They include bill language reflecting the conference committee's proposal for resolving the House and Senate differences on a bill, and the joint explanatory statement that explains the bill language.

For FY20 10, the earmark disclosure lists for six appropriations bills are included in the explanatory statement for H.R. 3288 (enacted as P.L. 111-117). That statement is contained in conference report H.Rept. 111-366 available at http:// frwebgate.access 1 1_cong_reports&docid=f:hr366. 11 1.pdf. The six bills are the Commerce-Justice-Science, Financial Services, Labor-HHS-Education, Military Construction-VA, State-Foreign Operations, and Transportation-HUD appropriations bills. The earmark disclosure lists for the other six FY20 10 bills are included in the explanatory statements for H.R. 2997 (P.L. 111-80, Agriculture), H.R. 3326 (P.L. 111-118, Defense), H.R. 3183 (P.L. 111-85, Energy-Water), H.R. 2892 (P.L. 111-83, Homeland Security), H.R. 2996 (P.L. 111- 88, Interior-Environment), and H.R. 2918 (P.L. 111-68, Legislative Branch).

For FY2009, the earmark disclosure lists for nine appropriations bills are included in the explanatory statement for H.R. 1105 (enacted as P.L. 111-8). That statement is contained in a committee print of the House Appropriations Committee, available at http://www.gpoaccess.gov/congress/. The nine bills are the Agriculture, Commerce-Justice-Science, Energy-Water, Financial Services, Interior-Environment, Labor-HHS Education, Legislative Branch, State-Foreign Operations, and Transportation-HUD appropriations bills. The earmark disclosure lists for the other three FY2009 bills are included in the explanatory statement for H.R. 2638 (enacted as P.L. 110-329). That statement is contained in a committee print of the House Appropriations Committee, available at *http://www.gpoaccess.gov/congress/house/appropriations/ 09conappro.html*. The three bills are the Defense, Homeland Security, and Military Construction-VA appropriations bills.

For FY2008, the earmark disclosure lists for all appropriations bills except Defense are contained in the explanatory statement for H.R. 2764 (enacted as P.L. 110-161). That statement is contained in a committee print of the House Appropriations Committee, available at http://www.gpoaccess.gov/congress. The earmark disclosure list for the FY2008 Defense bill is contained in the explanatory statement in the conference report on H.R. 3222 (enacted as P.L. 110-116).

4 In addition, the FY20 10 disclosure list for the Financial Services bill notes the Judiciary as a requester for five earmarks.

[5] For related discussion, see CRS Report RL34648, *Bush Administration Policy Regarding Congressionally Originated Earmarks: An Overview*, by Clinton T. Brass, Garrett Hatch, and R. Eric Petersen.

[6] No source comprehensively tracks subsequent actions that could have altered the number or value of earmarks disclosed by Congress.

[7] CRS Report 97-684, *The Congressional Appropriations Process: An Introduction*, by Sandy Streeter, pp. 15-16.

In: Earmarks: Disclosure, Legal Developments... ISBN: 978-1-61324-588-0
Editors: Roger D. Halstead

Chapter 6

TRANSPORTATION SPENDING UNDER AN EARMARK BAN

Robert S. Kirk, William J. Mallett and David Randall Peterman

SUMMARY

Earmarks—formally known as congressionally directed spending—have directed a significant amount of federal transportation spending in recent years. Proposals to ban earmarks in authorization and appropriations bills are under consideration in both houses of Congress. This report discusses how federal highway, transit, and aviation funding might be distributed under an earmark ban, and how members of Congress might influence the distribution.

Currently, about 80% of federal highway funds and 70% of transit funds are distributed by formulas set forth in statutes. The distribution of formula highway funds is under the control of the states. The bulk of formula transit funding is under the control of local governments and public transit agencies. Most federal funding for aviation is for operation of the air traffic control system and safety-related programs and is generally not earmarked. Most aviation infrastructure spending is distributed according to priorities set forth in national plans, but a small percentage is available for earmarking. Federal funding for maritime purposes is directed by statute and is not earmarked.

Most of the remaining federal transportation funding is distributed under discretionary programs. U.S. Department of Transportation (DOT) discretionary funds are typically distributed through a competitive grant-making process, within guidelines established by Congress and the department. In practice, however, much of this funding has been earmarked by Congress in recent years. The precise share of federal transportation dollars that is spent on earmarks cannot readily be calculated, but according to a DOT Inspector General report, in FY2006 approximately 13% of DOT's total budgetary resources were earmarked.

Banning earmarks would not eliminate the opportunity for members to direct the allocation of transportation resources. The funding formulas and eligibility rules in authorization bills can be shaped to favor particular states, congressional districts, and projects. "Soft" earmarks can be used to identify a project as a congressional priority in appropriations bill report language apparently without violating an earmark ban, based on current House and Senate rules, by not specifying an amount of funding. Without earmarking, members could continue to call or write DOT in support of projects. Members may also seek to influence the priority a project receives under mandated state and local planning procedures, which can increase the likelihood of federal funding without an earmark.

INTRODUCTION

Proposals in both the House and the Senate to ban earmarks may lead to changes in the way transportation funding decisions are made. This report explains what earmarks are and discusses their use in surface transportation finance. It then considers how federal highway, transit, and aviation funding might be distributed if such a ban goes into effect, and how members of Congress might influence the distribution.

Earmarks and the Structure of Federal Transportation Funding

The structure of federal transportation funding is typically determined in periodic transportation authorization legislation, which continues some existing programs (often with modifications) and creates new programs. The vast majority of funding is distributed directly to states, local governments, and transportation authorities by formulas that are set in these laws. Under the formula programs, the decisions about which projects get funded with that money are made by the states and local governments, subject to federal guidelines.

The authorization legislation also creates a number of discretionary (non-formula) transportation grant programs. These programs collectively distribute a relatively small portion of federal transportation funding. In theory, these programs award grants, at the discretion of the federal Department of Transportation (DOT), through a competitive application process.

Table 1. Congressionally Directed Spending Within the Department of Transportation, FY2006

	Number of Items	**Millions of Dollars**	**Percent of DOT's New Budget Authority**
Congressionally Directed Spending	8,056	$8,545	13.5
Authorization	6,474	N/A	N/A
Appropriation	1,582	N/A	N/A
DOT Agency	**Number of Items**	**Millions of Dollars**	**Percent of Agency's New Budget Authority**
Department of Transportation	8,056	$8,545	
Federal Highway Administration	6,556	$5,676	15.5
Federal Transit Administration	1,252	$2,406	28.0
Federal Aviation Administration	204	$408	2.8
Other	44	$56	1.5

Source: Office of the Inspector General, *Review of Congressional Earmarks Within Department of Transportation Programs*, Department of Transportation, "Report Number AV-2007-066," Washington, DC, September 7, 2007, http://www.oig.dot.gov/library-item/4256.

Note: N/A means not available. Table includes Congressionally Directed Spending that may not fall within the definition found in House and Senate rules. For example, data include 34 Federal Transit Administration (FTA) New Starts projects that passed through the New Starts program planning and evaluation process. These projects accounted for $1,370 million of the $1,500 million New Starts project budget in FY2006, according to the IG's report. Excluding these projects reduces the earmarked portion of FTA's budget to 12.0% and of DOT's budget to 11.3%. New budget authority is authority provided by federal law to enter into financial obligations that will result in immediate or future outlays involving federal government funds.

In recent years, funding for discretionary transportation grant programs has been heavily earmarked by Congress in the authorization legislation and in the annual DOT appropriations acts. In addition, Congress has on occasion earmarked portions of highway formula funding.[1]

The magnitude of transportation earmarking is difficult to estimate. Earmarks are found in both authorization and appropriations legislation, and while Congress has been identifying "earmarks and Congressionally directed spending items" in appropriations legislation since FY2008, those lists do not include earmarks found in the authorization legislation that might be funded in that fiscal year. DOT's Inspector General (IG) examined transportation earmarking in both the authorization and appropriations bills for FY2006 and estimated that 13.5% of total budget authority provided to DOT in that year was congressionally directed. The IG also estimated that 80% of the earmarks originated in the authorization and 20% in the appropriations bill (**Table 1**).

A major attraction of transportation earmarks to members is that they provide specific, identifiable benefits for constituents.[2] However, earmarks have not always been part of the transportation funding process. Even now, most of the Federal Aviation Administration (FAA) budget is free of earmarks, with the Airport Improvement Program's discretionary funding being the major exception.

Republican congressional leaders have expressed opposition to earmarks,[3] and press reports indicate that Republicans have voted to ban earmarking in the 112th Congress.[4] As Republicans will control the House of Representatives in the 112th Congress, this could mean that House bills will not contain earmarks. It is not clear that the Senate will follow the same practice. How legislators would deal with bills that contain Senate earmarks but not House earmarks is uncertain. Also, according to press reports, some members have suggested making exceptions to the earmark ban for certain types of projects, including transportation projects.[5]

WHAT IS A CONGRESSIONAL EARMARK?

The rules in both houses of Congress include identical definitions of "congressionally directed spending."[6] The rules define an earmark as

> a provision or report language included primarily at the request of a Senator [Representative] providing, authorizing, or recommending a specific amount of discretionary budget authority, credit authority, or other spending authority for a contract, loan, loan guarantee, grant, loan authority, or other expenditure with or to an entity, or targeted to a specific State, locality or Congressional district, other than through a statutory or administrative formula- driven or competitive award process.[7]

This definition covers earmarks in authorization and appropriations bills as well as in committee reports. Provisions in committee reports may not have the force of law but are often used to give guidance to executive branch departments. One example of such an earmark appeared in the conference committee's explanatory statement on the Omnibus Appropriations Act, 2009 (P.L. 111-8):

Account	Project	Amount	Requester(s)
Surface Transportation Priorities	Coalfields Expressway, WV	$4,750,000	Senator Byrd

The effect of an earmark ban based on a House rule might be limited, depending upon the specific rule.[8] This is because transportation appropriations bills in the House come to the floor under a Rules Committee resolution establishing the rules for consideration of the bill. The Rules Committee can and often does waive rules, and it might have the ability to waive a rule banning earmarks. Consequently, a ban based on a rule or on a rule-based definition of earmarks could be of limited effectiveness.[9] Also, in both the House and Senate, enforcement of a rule requires that a member stand and object to an identified violation by raising a point of order.[10] Some earmarks include the language "notwithstanding any other provision of law." This would circumvent even an earmark ban codified in law.

"Soft" Earmarks and "Hard" Earmarks

The term "congressionally directed spending item" under House and Senate rules appears to permit some "soft" transportation earmarks. Whereas "hard" earmarks specify the project place, purpose, and funding amount in bill or bill report language, "soft" earmarks do not specify the amount of funding.[11] Two types of soft earmarks are found in federal transportation finance: place naming and road naming.

Under place naming, the project place is named in the bill or report language, but no funding amount is designated. The appropriators direct the agency to give priority to grant applications from the named places. This form of congressional designation has been most commonly used to influence Airport Improvement Program (AIP) spending. For example, in the FY1990 Department of Transportation Appropriations bill, the House conference report (H. Rept. 101- 183) urged the Federal Aviation Administration (FAA) to give priority to

> grant applications involving the construction or further development of the following airports:
> Akron-Canton Regional Airport, Ohio.
> Alexander Hamilton Airport, Virgin Islands ...

By not designating the amount, place naming appears not to be covered by the definition of earmarks under current House and Senate rules.[12]

Road naming is similar to but has been used less often than place naming. The Surface Transportation Assistance Act of 1982 (P.L. 97-424; H.Rept. 97-987) directed the states to give priority in use of federal highway funds to the primary routes designated in a particular committee print.[13]

The definition of an earmark in congressional rules also appears to exclude most of the Federal Transit Administration's (FTA's) New Starts and Small Starts Program funding. [14] Congress appropriates amounts for specific projects each year, but these projects have previously been chosen through a competitive, multi-step approval process that is administered by FTA according to law. However, appropriators sometimes add projects to this list, and these additional projects may fall within the definition of earmark in House and Senate rules.[15]

New Starts and Small Starts projects are also specifically named in surface transportation authorization legislation, but this does not guarantee funding. The surface transportation authorization bills merely make projects eligible for consideration in the competitive new starts process. This applies even in cases where a dollar amount is assigned because the law specifically states that these authorizations are subject to the new starts process. [16] Moreover, because funds for New Starts projects come from the general fund, not the highway trust fund, an appropriation is necessary once a project has been approved through DOT's process.

EARMARKING OF SURFACE TRANSPORTATION FUNDING

Extensive earmarking of surface transportation programs is a relatively recent phenomenon. It has been common in authorizations since FY1992 and for appropriations only since FY2001.

The House rule establishing a separate Committee on Roads, adopted on June 2, 1913, included a point of order against any provision for a specific road. According to an analysis by *Transportation Weekly*, the rule was reasonably effective in preventing the earmarking of highway projects until the 1970s, when the House Rules Committee began waiving the rule on earmarks within larger transportation bills.[17] However, highway earmarks in the authorization and appropriations bills were few in number until the late 1 980s. The increase to 152 earmarks in the Surface Transportation and Uniform Relocation Assistance Act of 1987 (P.L. 100-17), up from 10 under the 1982 Act, elicited a presidential veto and President Ronald Reagan's comment that "I haven't seen this much lard since I handed out blue ribbons at the Iowa State Fair." Congress overrode the veto.[18]

The number of highway earmarks grew in each of the three next surface transportation authorization acts to a high of 5,671 in the Safe, Accountable, Flexible, Efficient Transportation Equity Act: A Legacy for Users (SAFETEA; P.L. 109-59), enacted in 2005.[19] Annual appropriations bill highway earmarks were still under 50 per year through FY1990, and there were none in the FY1996-FY1998 period.[20] However, the number of highway earmarks in appropriations bills grew quickly from 96 in FY2000 to 614 in FY2010.[21] The House ban on highway earmarks was repealed in 1999.

THE ROLE OF DOT IN PROJECT SPENDING

DOT is responsible for the administration of the transportation programs of the federal government. Most of that funding is distributed under formula programs, with projects selected by states, local governments, or transportation authorities pursuant to a federally mandated planning process at the state and local levels. DOT's direct involvement in project selection is mostly limited to the unearmarked funding in the department's discretionary programs.

Highways

Over 80% of the highway funding in SAFETEA, the most recent surface transportation authorization act, is distributed through formula programs.[22] These funds are under the control of the states.

Much of the remaining 20% of highway funding is distributed through discretionary programs, such as the Transportation, Community, and System Preservation Program, the National Corridor Infrastructure Improvement Program, or the Interstate Maintenance Discretionary Program. The Federal Highway Administration (FHWA) administers a competitive grant selection process for discretionary programs, except to the extent that spending under these programs is directed by earmarks. In practice, most of the money available under these programs has been earmarked in recent years.

Whether for discretionary or formula program projects, federal law requires that all highway projects must be a product of the planning process under the auspices of a Metropolitan Planning Organization or the state DOT. The projects must be included in the State Transportation Improvement Plan (STIP). The STIP lists the state's highway projects, often in priority order. To be eligible for federal highway funding, either discretionary or formula, the project must be on the STIP.

Transit and Rail

Like highway funding, most federal transit funding is distributed by statutory funding formulas. Under current law about 70% of the roughly $10 billion annual budget is distributed in this way. To be eligible for federal funds, transit projects must be included in a Transportation Improvement Program approved by a Metropolitan Planning Organization. Unlike federal highway funding, most of which flows to the states, most transit funding flows directly to local transit authorities. Only transit funds designated for urbanized areas with populations of 200,000 people or less and non-urbanized (rural) areas are administered by the states. Under the formula programs, such as the Urbanized Area Formula Grant Program and the Fixed Guideway Modernization Program, FTA simply administers the funds and does not select projects.

Two major programs overseen by FTA are not governed by formula: the New Starts and Small Starts program ($2.0 billion in FY20 10) and the Bus and Bus Facilities program ($982 million).[23]

In the case of the New Starts and Small Starts programs, FTA allocates funding based on factors determined in authorization legislation.[24] Bus and Bus Facilities program funding is largely allocated according to earmarks.

As with other DOT modes, the majority of intercity rail funding in the Federal Railroad Administration (FRA) has not been earmarked. The two largest FRA programs are support for Amtrak and the High Speed and Intercity Passenger Rail (HSIPR) Program. Amtrak receives both operating and capital support; the expenditure of these funds is determined by Amtrak (though Amtrak's capital spending is focused in the Northeast, where most of the infrastructure that it owns is located). The HSIPR program began in FY2010 and is a competitive grant program that has not been earmarked.

Aviation

Aviation authorization bills are generally not earmarked. Appropriations bills have in recent years had some FAA discretionary funding earmarked, and in the 1990s some appropriations bills "place named" airports for Airport Improvement Program (AIP) funding.

The (AIP) is both a formula and a discretionary grant program. Generally about two-thirds of funding is distributed as "entitlements" through formulas set forth in the reauthorization bill. Airport projects must be part of the national Airport Capital Improvement Plan, which is developed by the FAA, airport sponsors, states, and planning agencies. This planning process culminates in a list of priority projects. FAA oversees the distribution of AIP entitlement funds and enforces compliance with the eligibility criteria. Unlike the Federal-Aid Highway Program, federal aid to airports flows directly to the airport sponsor, usually an airport authority.

AIP discretionary funds are used by the FAA to fund priority projects through a competitive grant process. In recent years, AIP discretionary funds have often been earmarked substantially. Earmarking moves an airport up the priority list and provides funding. The discretionary funds are also subject to set-asides for nationwide priorities set by Congress, such as the 35% noise set-aside and the 4% Military Airport Program set-aside.

Recently, some earmarks have also appeared in the Facilities and Equipment component of the FAA budget. The most significant of these have been for projects under FAA's Tower/Terminal Air Traffic Control Program and the Instrument Landing Systems Program. The priorities for spending under these programs also are established through a national planning process.

According to DOT's inspector general, earmarking has delayed some projects assigned high priority through this process while funding lower-priority projects.[25]

Maritime

DOT's Federal Maritime Administration provides support for certain maritime operations and vessel construction, typically under criteria set by law. Most capital programs to benefit marine transportation, such as harbor dredging and lock repair, are undertaken by other federal agencies, notably the U.S. Army Corps of Engineers, rather than by DOT.

TRANSPORTATION SPENDING UNDER AN EARMARK BAN

Both highways and transit are included in a single multi-year surface transportation authorization bill, which establishes programs and sets authorized spending levels.[26] In the House, both the highway and transit sections of the bill are developed primarily by the Highways and Transit Subcommittee of the Transportation and Infrastructure Committee (T&I), although the full committee also takes an active role. In the Senate, the Environment and Public Works Committee has jurisdiction over the highway provisions, while the Banking, Housing, and Urban Affairs Committee handles transit. Provisions involving highway trust fund and revenue issues are under the jurisdiction of the Ways and Means Committee in the House and the Committee on Finance in the Senate. Aviation reauthorization bills are primarily under the jurisdiction of the T&I Committee in the House and the Commerce, Science, and Transportation Committee in the Senate.

For appropriations legislation, highways, transit, and aviation are under the jurisdiction of the appropriations committees in each house. Members of the appropriations committees also oversee the implementation of federal transportation spending through hearings that provide the opportunity to publicly call the attention of DOT officials to issues that are important to the member's state or district.

The process of developing a transportation authorization bill typically begins with a schedule of hearings in which members can participate, and at which local officials promoting the need for particular projects can testify. Once the bill is introduced, members may discuss their concerns with the committee (both at the member and staff levels). Such discussions may continue through the bill markup and even during the eventual floor debate.[27] An earmark ban would not affect the ability of members and their staffs to engage in such discussions. Nor would it limit their ability to correspond and meet with DOT officials in support of projects.

A ban on transportation earmarks would affect principally discretionary programs overseen by DOT. It would likely have little direct impact on the formula programs that make up most federal transportation funding.

Earmarks serve as a way for members of Congress to ensure that discretionary transportation funds are distributed according to their priorities, rather than those of the Administration. If earmarks are prohibited, and if Congress does not act in other ways to set funding priorities within the discretionary programs, then the job of setting priorities would be left to DOT, subject to the grant selection criteria set forth in law and regulation. One alternative to earmarks would be more detailed legislative language to govern the allocation of funds.

Divergences between congressional and Administration priorities for transportation funding have come to the fore on several recent occasions. In FY2007, a year in which Congress passed a yearlong continuing resolution and the appropriators did not earmark the discretionary programs, the George W. Bush Administration decided to consolidate virtually all discretionary funds in the highway and transit programs to advance its focus on comprehensive congestion mitigation strategies in metropolitan areas through urban partnership agreements. The roughly $850 million in discretionary funding was divided among just five cities.[28] This amount included unallocated discretionary bus program funds that had been divided among hundreds of projects by Congress in the previous fiscal year.[29]

Similarly, the Obama Administration used unallocated FY2009 Bus and Bus Facilities funds to support one of its policy priorities, "livability."[30] Livability, which involves providing alternatives to the car and integrating transportation, housing, and environmental policies, was not specifically established as a policy priority by Congress.

An earmark ban would elevate the visibility of the programmatic selection process and of the selection criteria, which may be established by Congress. Under the proposed earmark ban, other traditional avenues for members of Congress to influence the flow of transportation funding could become more important, such as involvement in the policymaking aspects of transportation budgeting and interaction with both federal and state transportation officials. Increased reliance on formula funding may make it more critical for members to make sure that projects of importance to their constituents are included in transportation plans at an acceptable priority level.[31]

Members of the appropriations committees can improve the chances that a specific project will be funded without earmarking by increasing the amount of funding provided to a particular program.[32] Members also have the opportunity to include provisions in appropriations legislation that may affect transportation program expenditures, including project selection, without identifying specific projects.[33]

How an Earmark-Free Highways Program Might Work

The total size of the Federal-Aid Highway Program has the largest impact on spending at the state and local levels. Reauthorization bills may extend existing programs, create new or revised programs, or allow programs to lapse. Typically, members may support increased spending for programs that are more important to their state or district relative to other programs. For example, a member from a state or district with a large number of deficient bridges might give priority to increased funding of the Highway Bridge Program.

In the absence of earmarks, highway program formulas may become more important in directing the flow of highway funding. For example, the Transportation Equity Act for the 21st Century (TEA-21; P.L. 105-178) added factors based on states annual contributions to the highway account of the Highway Trust Fund to two programs' funding formulas. This directed money toward states whose motorists paid larger amounts of highway taxes and away from states whose motorists paid relatively less in highway taxes.

A provision in SAFETEA, the "Equity Bonus Program," makes the impact of a ban on earmarks difficult to gauge. The Equity Bonus funding distribution functions as an overlay on other highway programs, and is meant to assure that all states receive a share of highway funding equal to at least a specified proportion of their motorists' payments into the highway trust fund.

If the Equity Bonus Program is reauthorized, earmarks under the High Priority Project Program, the largest single source of earmarks, may not change the total any state receives of highway formula funds and High Priority Project Program funds combined. For example, SAFETEA included over 5,000 earmarks under the High Priority Project program, but these earmarks reduced Equity Bonus funding by equivalent amounts and left each state's total under these programs unchanged. Consequently, a ban on earmarks under these programs would not necessarily affect the total flow of federal highway funds to any state, nor would it necessarily affect the total amount of federal spending for highways. However, an earmark ban might affect the flow of highway funds to individual congressional districts, as the Equity Bonus Program does not assure spending at the district level. Earmarks of funds from discretionary programs not affected by the Equity Bonus Program could increase a state's total federal highway funding.

Transit and Rail Programs without Earmarks

Like the highways programs, most federal transit programs rely heavily on funding formulas established in authorization laws. Formulas are not a neutral way of distributing funds, as the way in which a formula is constructed and subsequently modified can have significant effects on the allocation of funding. For example, in the 1980s transit funding dedicated to fixed guideway modernization was distributed by DOT based on an administrative formula that sent most funds to transit rail systems that existed before the creation of the federal transit program in 1964. This administrative formula was altered and inserted into law in 1991 in part to widen the distribution of funds to include rail systems built in the 1970s and 1 980s. This change was reinforced by modifications made to the formula in the surface authorization law passed in 1997.

The New Starts and Small Starts Program, which supports construction of rail and bus transit projects, is a particular source of misunderstanding with respect to earmarking. Under current law, a transit project must be specifically mentioned in the authorization legislation in order to be eligible for federal support. However, being named in the legislation does not assure any level of funding, and does not guarantee that the project will be funded at all. Thus, inclusion in the legislation does not constitute earmarking under the current definition adopted by Congress. An earmark ban would not alter the need to include a specific transit project in the authorization bill if its sponsors hope to receive federal assistance.

The allocation of funding among the various transit programs may become even more important in the absence of earmarks. For example, districts with rail transit systems are likely to do well when more funds are dedicated to the Fixed-Guideway Modernization Program. Rural districts, by contrast, are likely to do well when more funding goes to the Non-Urbanized Area Formula Program. FTA also administers the Bus and Bus Facilities Program, which has been heavily earmarked in the past. In the event of an earmark ban, funding under this program presumably would be distributed according to FTA criteria, and Congress may want to provide FTA with guidance in developing those criteria.

An earmark ban will not make much difference in the realm of intercity passenger rail because, as noted earlier, these funding programs have not been earmarked.

Aviation Programs without Earmarks

An earmark ban would be less significant for aviation than for surface transportation, due to the relatively minor role of earmarking in aviation funding. An earmark ban would not necessarily affect the ability of members to increase the priority given particular projects in the Airport Capital Improvement Plan. Alternatively, members may seek to adjust the entitlement formulas in the Airport Improvement Program in ways that might benefit particular airports.

In the absence of earmarking, members whose states or districts have particular concerns about noise mitigation or conversion of a military airfield to civilian or dual use could support increases in the set-asides for those purposes, increasing the likelihood that a particular project will be funded without naming the project. Members could also intervene in the process of setting priorities for FAA facilities and equipment expenditures under the Tower/Terminal Air Traffic Control Program and the Instrument Landing Systems Program.

One of the federal government's more visible aviation programs, the Essential Air Service Program, subsidizes commercial flights to airports that lost service under airline deregulation. This program is not earmarked, although Congress has from time to time altered the criteria that determine whether a particular airport is eligible for the program.

End Notes

[1] The appropriators deducted an across-the-board percentage of contract authority from the major highway formula programs for earmarking in FY2004, FY2005, and FY2006. See "Coming in FY2007—No Highway Earmarks?," *Transportation Weekly*, January 25, 2006, p. 3.

[2] David A. Fahrenthold, "Between Losing and Going Home: the House Basement," *Washington Post*, December 9, 2010, pp. A1, A22. Historically, earmark funding has not been made

available in equal amounts to all members of Congress in transportation legislation. Committee leadership decides how and in what amounts earmark funding is distributed. See "In-Depth Analysis: Earmarked Highway Projects: Their History, Their Nature and Their Role in Highway Legislation," *Transportation Weekly,* v. 3, issue 24, April 10, 2002, pp. 4, 10-12. See also "TW Analysis: Above the Line Highway Earmarks," *Transportation Weekly*, v. 7, issue 10, January 17, 2006, pp. 1-10.

[3] Office of Representative John Boehner, "House & Senate GOP Leaders United on Earmark Ban," press release, November 15, 2010, http://www.johnboehner.house.gov/News/DocumentSingle.aspx?DocumentID=214878.

[4] Brian Faler, "House Republicans Vote to Continue Ban on U.S. Budget 'Earmarks,'" *Business Week*, November 18, 2010, http://www.businessweek.com/news/2010-11-18/house-republicans-vote- and Stephen Dinan, "With Ban, GOP Calls Duel on Earmarks," *Washington Times*, March 12, 2010, http://www.washingtontimes.com/news/2010/mar/12/with-yearlong-ban-house-gop-throws

[5] Jane Sherman, "GOP Gets Queasy Over Earmark Ban," *Politico*, December 9, 2010, http://www.politico.com/news/ stories/1210/46172.html.

[6] See CRS Report RL34462, *House and Senate Procedural Rules Concerning Earmark Disclosure*, by Sandy Streeter, for a more detailed discussion.

[7] House Rule XXI, clause 9 (e), http://www.rules. Senate Rule XLIV, clause 5 (a), http://rules.senate.gov/public/index.cfm?p=RuleXLIV. An earmark ban could be established in law or in the rules of the House and Senate.

[8] CRS Report 98-313, *House Rules Committee Hearings on Special Rules*, by Megan Suzanne Lynch.

[9] For example, see H.Res. 184, 111th Congress, first session.

[10] CRS Report 98-306, *Points of Order, Rulings, and Appeals in the Senate*, by Valerie Heitshusen.

[11] The terms "hard" and "soft" earmarks are terms of convenience, often used by congressional staff, but have no statutory meaning. Historically, soft earmarks included congressionally directed project spending not listed in the text of the bill itself, but listed in the language of the accompanying report. The current earmark definitions, however, include such designations, making them "hard" earmarks under the House and Senate rules.

[12] The FY1994 Transportation Appropriations Conference Report (H.Rept. 103-3 00) included language in which the conferees rejected the place name lists in the House and Senate reports arguing that the process was "neither effective at ensuring funding nor useful at identifying those airports with the highest need for federal assistance." Significant place naming of airports, however, reappeared in the conference report of the FY2000 Transportation Appropriations Act (H.Rept. 106-3 55). In the FY2001 Transportation Appropriations conference report (H.Rept. 106-940) amounts were specified, effectively making the designations "hard" earmarks.

[13] "One Possible Way Around an Earmark Ban," *Transportation Weekly*, vol. 12, no. 4 (November 18, 2010), p. 9. For a discussion of report language earmarks and why the federal Department of Transportation responds to them, see "White House Considers a Ban on Most FY2007 Earmarks," *Transportation Weekly*, vol. 9, no. 8 (January 17, 2008), pp. 1-2.

[14] The appropriations conference report earmark lists, however, appear to list all New Starts and Small Starts projects.

[15] Office of the Inspector General, *Review of Congressional Earmarks Within Department of Transportation Programs*, Department of Transportation, "Report Number AV-2007-066," Washington, DC, September 7, 2007, pp. 11, 15-17, http://www.oig.dot.gov/library-item/4256.

[16] See section 3043 of the Safe, Accountable, Flexible, Efficient Transportation Equity Act: A Legacy for Users (SAFETEA), P.L. 109-59.

[17] "The Last Rule Banning Earmarks," *Transportation Weekly*, vol. 12, no. 3 (November 10, 2010), p. 13.

[18] Federal Highway Administration, *President Ronald Reagan and the Surface Transportation and Uniform Relocation Assistance Act of 1987*, Washington, DC, November 23, 2010, http://www.fhwa.dot.gov/infrastructure

[19] "Congress Completes Work on Highway Bill," *Transportation Weekly*, vol. 6, no. 34 (August 4, 2005), p. 19.

[20] "In-Depth Analysis: Earmarked Highway Projects: Their History, Their Nature and Their Role in Highway Legislation," *Transportation Weekly*, vol. 3, no. 24 (April 10, 2002), pp. 1, 3-11. *Transportation Weekly*'s earmark totals are used here because they provide a consistent source of earmark analysis over time. The tallies are unofficial. CRS has not verified the counts.

[21] Federal funding for transportation was provided in FY2007 under a year-long continuing resolution that did not contain earmarks.

[22] The elimination of the High Priority Projects program, which is all earmarks, could increase the percent of the Federal-Aid Highway Program that is distributed by formula.

[23] U.S. Department of Transportation, Federal Transit Administration, "FTA Supplemental Fiscal Year 2010 Apportionments, Allocations, and Corrections," 75 *Federal Register*, 27056-27109, May 13, 2010, http://www.fta.dot.gov/documents/2010-11479.pdf.

[24] Congress has been listing all projects funded through the New Starts/Small Starts program in the "Earmarks and Congressionally Directed Spending Items" table for DOT appropriations bills, although by the definition of earmark provided in the rule it is not clear that many of the projects should be in that table, since many are the result of "a statutory or administrative ... competitive award process." For example, in FY20 10, only $136 million was appropriated for projects added by Congress to the list of recommended projects submitted by FTA, 7% of the total program appropriation.

[25] Office of the Inspector General, *Review of Congressional Earmarks Within Department of Transportation Programs*, "Report Number AV-2007-066," Washington, DC, September 7, 2007, p. 12.

[26] After TEA2 1 expired, Congress passed twelve "stop-gap" extensions for a period of almost two years until SAFETEA (in effect, a five-year bill) was enacted on August 10, 2005.

[27] The Department of Transportation usually also drafts a suggested bill. The DOT bill is introduced by request in both the House and Senate.

[28] "DOT Urban Partnership Awards a Far Cry from Usual Earmarking," *Transportation Weekly*, vol. 8, no. 32 (September 5, 2007), pp. 3-4.

[29] U.S. Department of Transportation, Federal Transit Administration, "Announcement of Project Selections for FY2007 Discretionary Programs," 72 *Federal Register*, 47123-47125, August 22, 2007, http://edocket.access.gpo.gov/ 2007/pdf/07-4125.pdf; U.S. Department of Transportation, Federal Transit Administration, "FTA Fiscal Year 2006 Apportionments and Allocations," 70 *Federal Register*, 75648-75709, December 20, 2005, http://www.fta.dot.gov/ documents/05-24154.pdf.

[30] U.S. Department of Transportation, Federal Transit Administration, "Section 5309 Bus and Bus Facilities Livability Initiative Program Grants," 74 *Federal Register*, 64984-64989, December 8, 2009, http://edocket.access pdf/E9-29242.pdf.

[31] Implementation procedures for an earmark ban could tighten the working definition. For example, see House Republican Conference, *Earmark Moratorium Guidance*, March 16, 2010.

[32] SAFETEA included guaranteed funding levels which in effect allowed appropriators to increase funding over the guaranteed amount but not lower funding below these amounts. Changing the funding for any program changes the relative distribution.

[33] For example, for several years appropriations acts have included a provision barring FTA from signing full-funding grant agreements for New Starts projects that request more than a 60% federal share, although by statute the federal share can be up to 80%.

INDEX

A

access, 75, 92
accommodation, 42
accounting, 63
agencies, viii, 5, 12, 29, 31, 33, 34, 36, 39, 40, 41, 42, 43, 44, 45, 46, 61, 77, 85, 86
agency decisions, 35
air traffic control system, 77
airports, 82, 85, 90, 91
appropriations, vii, viii, ix, 1, 3, 4, 6, 7, 9, 11, 12, 14, 15, 17, 19, 20, 26, 27, 28, 29, 30, 31, 33, 34, 35, 36, 40, 41, 44, 49, 50, 51, 52, 53, 54, 55, 56, 57, 58, 59, 61, 63, 66, 67, 71, 72, 73, 74, 75, 77, 78, 80, 81, 83, 85, 86, 88, 91, 92
authorities, 78, 83, 84
authority, 2, 10, 20, 30, 34, 36, 37, 38, 39, 41, 44, 51, 57, 80, 81, 85, 90

B

ban, ix, 77, 78, 80, 81, 83, 87, 88, 89, 90, 91, 92
base, 36, 43
beneficiaries, 2, 10, 21
benefits, 2, 3, 11, 19, 20, 27, 29, 80
budgetary resources, 78

C

capital programs, 86
case law, 42, 44
certification, viii, 4, 11, 14, 17, 18, 23, 24, 25, 30, 31
cities, 87
collateral, 23, 31
commercial, 90
commodity, 57
communication, 34, 35, 36
competitive grant program, 85
compliance, 14, 23, 34, 36, 37, 85
conception, 39, 44
conditioning, 29
conference, vii, viii, 1, 3, 5, 6, 9, 10, 11, 13, 14, 17, 18, 19, 20, 21, 22, 23, 24, 25, 26, 27, 28, 29, 30, 34, 35, 37, 43, 75, 81, 82, 91
conference committees, 5, 13, 34, 37
Conference Report, 26, 29, 31, 75, 91
confidentiality, 36
confrontation, 44
congress, 75
Congress, viii, ix, 5, 6, 7, 13, 17, 19, 27, 29, 30, 31, 33, 34, 35, 37, 38, 39, 40, 41, 42, 43, 44, 45, 46, 49, 50, 51, 52, 53, 54, 58, 59, 60, 61, 62, 63, 64, 67, 73, 74, 76, 77, 78, 80, 82, 83, 85, 87, 89, 90, 91, 92
consent, 24, 30
constituents, 80, 88
Constitution, 6, 37, 40

construction, 43, 61, 82, 86, 89
consulting, 36
controversial, 37
cost, viii, 33, 34, 36, 39
covering, 42
criticism, 39

D

decision-making process, 43
Department of Defense, 30, 61
Department of Transportation (DOT), 77, 78, 79, 80, 82, 83, 84, 85, 86, 87, 89, 91, 92
deregulation, 90
directives, 34, 37, 42
disclosure, vii, viii, 1, 2, 3, 5, 6, 7, 9, 10, 11, 13, 14, 15, 17, 18, 19, 20, 22, 23, 25, 26, 27, 49, 50, 51, 52, 53, 55, 56, 57, 59, 60, 61, 63, 67, 70, 71, 72, 73, 74, 75
distribution, ix, 38, 50, 55, 77, 78, 85, 88, 89, 92
distribution function, 88

E

eligibility criteria, 2, 10, 21, 85
employees, 36
enforcement, 81
equilibrium, 39
equipment, 90
equity, 36
ethics, 6, 14, 31
exclusion, 2, 10, 21
execution, 52
executive branch, 34, 35, 37, 40, 42, 43, 44, 45, 52, 81
Executive Order, viii, 5, 7, 12, 14, 29, 33, 34, 36, 37, 39, 40, 42, 44, 45, 46
executive orders, 37, 39, 40, 42
executive power, 37
exercise, 39
expenditures, 36, 88, 90

F

FAA, 80, 82, 85, 90
faith, 41
federal agency, 50, 51
federal aid, 85
federal assistance, 89, 91
federal funds, 84
federal government, viii, 33, 34, 80, 83, 90
Federal Highway Administration (FHWA), 79, 84, 92
federal law, 80, 84
Federal Register, 92
financial, viii, 4, 6, 11, 13, 17, 18, 19, 25, 31, 80
flexibility, 41, 42
flights, 90
food, 57
force, 37, 40, 44, 45, 81
formula, 2, 10, 20, 51, 77, 78, 79, 80, 81, 83, 84, 85, 87, 88, 89, 90, 92
funding, ix, 4, 12, 15, 28, 29, 37, 43, 45, 51, 52, 53, 54, 58, 66, 77, 78, 79, 80, 81, 82, 83, 84, 85, 86, 87, 88, 89, 90, 91, 92

G

General Accounting Office (GAO), 41
governments, 79
grant programs, 79, 80
grants, 34, 35, 79
growth, 72
GSA, 60, 70
guidance, 5, 12, 13, 31, 81, 90
guidelines, 78, 79

H

Hamilton, Alexander, 82
Health and Human Services (HHS), 44, 52, 54, 55, 56, 57, 60, 61, 62, 63, 65, 68, 75

highways, 86, 89
history, 40, 41, 42, 43, 45
House, vii, viii, 1, 2, 3, 4, 5, 6, 7, 9, 10, 11, 14, 17, 18, 19, 20, 21, 22, 23, 24, 25, 26, 27, 28, 29, 30, 31, 35, 43, 49, 50, 51, 57, 67, 75, 78, 79, 80, 81, 82, 83, 86, 90, 91, 92
House Report, 43
housing, 87
Housing and Urban Development (HUD), 52, 54, 55, 57, 60, 61, 62, 63, 64, 68, 75

I

identification, viii, 4, 11, 17, 18, 20, 49, 51
imports, 20
infrastructure, 77, 85, 92
injury, iv
intelligence, 15, 26
Iowa, 83
issues, 86

J

judicial interpretation, 38
jurisdiction, vii, 1, 4, 5, 9, 11, 12, 13, 15, 18, 25, 26, 57, 86

L

laws, viii, 33, 34, 35, 37, 40, 44, 78, 89
lead, 78
leadership, 91
legislation, vii, viii, 1, 3, 4, 6, 9, 11, 12, 15, 20, 21, 22, 25, 29, 30, 33, 34, 35, 40, 44, 49, 51, 52, 78, 79, 80, 82, 85, 86, 88, 89, 91
legislative proposals, 36
local government, 77, 78, 83

M

magnitude, 56, 63, 80
majority, 20, 21, 23, 27, 30, 37, 38, 61, 78, 85
manufacturing, 20
materials, 14
matter, 23, 28, 38, 41, 42, 43, 45
metropolitan areas, 87
military, 45, 61, 90
misunderstanding, 89
modernization, 89
modifications, 28, 78, 89

N

naming, 82, 90, 91
National Institutes of Health, 44
national security, 15, 26
neutral, 89
New Starts program, 79

O

Obama, 87
Office of Management and Budget, 35, 39, 44
Office of the Inspector General, 79, 91, 92
officials, 86, 87
Omnibus Appropriations Act,, 81
operations, 86
overlay, 88

P

parliamentary procedure, 21
permission, iv
permit, 41, 42, 81
Philadelphia, 46
policy, viii, 4, 5, 12, 19, 29, 33, 34, 36, 39, 40, 43, 44, 87
policy issues, 39

precedent, 44
precedents, 28
President, viii, 33, 34, 36, 37, 38, 39, 40, 42, 43, 44, 50, 52, 57, 58, 59, 60, 61, 63, 67, 68, 69, 70, 73, 74, 83, 92
Presidential Administration, 46
presidential authority, 38, 39, 44, 45
principles, 37, 39
profit, 4
project, viii, 27, 28, 31, 33, 34, 50, 51, 61, 78, 79, 81, 82, 83, 84, 88, 89, 90, 91
proposition, 2, 42
publishing, 51

R

raw materials, 20
reasoning, 38
recognition, 41
regulations, 39
relief, 2, 21
repair, 86
requirements, vii, viii, 1, 3, 4, 5, 7, 9, 11, 12, 13, 14, 18, 19, 20, 22, 23, 24, 25, 26, 29, 40, 51, 53, 75
resolution, 14, 15, 81, 87, 92
resources, 41, 78
response, 23, 27
restrictions, 4, 12, 24, 29, 40, 41, 42
revenue, 2, 10, 20, 21, 27, 86
routes, 82
rules, vii, viii, 1, 2, 3, 4, 5, 6, 9, 10, 11, 12, 13, 14, 17, 18, 19, 20, 21, 22, 24, 25, 30, 49, 50, 51, 53, 57, 75, 78, 79, 80, 81, 82, 91

S

safety, 77
scope, 29, 39, 46
seizure, 37, 38
Senate, vii, viii, 1, 2, 3, 6, 7, 9, 10, 11, 12, 13, 14, 15, 17, 18, 19, 20, 21, 23, 24, 25, 26, 27, 28, 29, 30, 31, 43, 49, 50, 51, 57, 75, 78, 79, 80, 81, 82, 86, 91, 92
Small Starts program, 84, 85, 92
spending, vii, viii, ix, 2, 5, 10, 13, 14, 17, 18, 19, 20, 25, 26, 27, 28, 29, 34, 36, 37, 40, 41, 50, 51, 57, 77, 80, 81, 82, 84, 85, 86, 88, 89, 91
state, ix, 13, 14, 20, 30, 36, 49, 51, 78, 83, 84, 86, 87, 88
State of the Union address, 36
states, viii, 5, 13, 14, 15, 33, 34, 35, 37, 40, 44, 51, 77, 78, 82, 83, 84, 85, 88, 90
statutes, 41, 44, 45, 77
steel, 37, 39
structure, 78
Supreme Court, 37, 40, 42, 43, 44
suspensions, 20

T

T&I, 86
tariff, vii, viii, 1, 2, 3, 4, 6, 9, 10, 11, 14, 19, 20, 25, 27, 29
tax deduction, 2, 10, 20, 21
taxes, 88
throws, 91
tissue, 44
tracks, 76
transparency, vii, viii, 2, 10, 17, 18, 19, 21, 26, 49, 51
transportation, ix, 77, 78, 79, 80, 81, 82, 83, 84, 86, 87, 88, 90, 91, 92
treatment, 39
trust fund, 82, 86, 88
TVA, 40

U

U.S. Army Corps of Engineers, 86
uniform, 2, 10, 21, 43, 44
United, 3, 6, 11, 20, 35, 36, 37, 41, 45, 46, 91

urban, 87

V

vacancies, 24
veto, 36, 83
vote, 10, 11, 13, 18, 21, 23, 24, 27, 28, 29, 30, 36, 91
voting, 43

W

waiver, 23, 24, 30
Washington, 6, 13, 31, 79, 90, 91, 92
White House, 91
workers, 37